FIRST,
THE GOOD NEWS

THE POSITIVE TRUTH ABOUT GOD, THE GOSPEL,
AND WHAT IT REALLY MEANS TO BE GAY

To Becky.

See page #248 —

You always have a place in my heart

Jim

FIRST,
THE GOOD NEWS

THE POSITIVE TRUTH ABOUT GOD, THE GOSPEL,
AND WHAT IT REALLY MEANS TO BE GAY

BY BISHOP JIM SWILLEY

FIRST, THE GOOD NEWS: The Positive Truth About God, The Gospel, And What It Really Means To Be Gay
ISBN 978-0-9787170-4-9
Copyright © 2012 by Jim Earl Swilley
Printer: United Book Press
Cover designer: Chris Haler
Front cover photo by Jonah Swilley
Back cover photo by B.J. Bueford
Published by Church In The Now Publishing, www.churchinthenow.org

TABLE OF CONTENTS

ACKNOWLEDGMENTS

To René Babcock: You've helped me with all of my books through the years, but dealing with the material contained here was no doubt a little beyond your comfort zone, to say the least. Thank you for your professionalism and unwavering support in this very different project. You never judged and never made me second-guess any of it, and for that I love you now more than ever!

To Pastor Avery Rogers: Many people say they are called... some people prove that they are called. You said that God called you and assigned you to me, personally, and I believe you. You've proven it like no other. Thanks for everything. I love you!

To Howard Blount: Howie, you've been an important part of my life since we were boys, but your help and feedback throughout this whole project has probably been your greatest gift to me. So much of what is here is the fruit of a thousand conversations we have had and, more times than I can count, you helped resuscitate it when it was on life-support. Thanks, bubba, for everything!

To David VanCronkhite: Man, you just would not give up on that GOOD NEWS thing! Your consistent, prophetic voice in my life shaped this book more than you know!

To Ken: We met just as I was finishing up the book, but you put the period at the end of the sentence and confirmed it all. Thanks for living out the words 'I love you!' in everything you say and do...

FOREWORD

I recently heard that the two most important days of your life are the day that you were born and the day you realize the reason you were born. The day I met and fell in love with Jimearl, I discovered the reason I was born. I deeply felt that we were meant to be together and we would be world changers. Gandhi said, "Be the change you want to see"... and we have been.

One of the things I have loved and continue to love about JE is the fact that he stays true to the truth God gives him. I believe he was purposefully kept out of the 'mainstream' to keep his message pure and uncontaminated. God's mercy, grace and unconditional love are the foundation for all that he teaches. I always believed God to be 'that good,' and when JE came into my life, he confirmed what was always in my heart and he has confirmed that for thousands of others over the years.

The truths that are contained in the words to follow have been lived out...with honor and integrity. I am so proud of the amazing man that has come forth like a beautiful butterfly. That's what Love does...it allows those in your life to be themselves—without judgment or condemnation—to become all they were Divinely created to be.

When you truly love someone unconditionally, you want them to be happy and fulfilled...even if it means that their life doesn't include you. Of course, I am still an integral part of JE's life and always will be...but I had to love him enough to let him go so he could experience all that he had dreamed.

My prayer is that you will read this with the eyes of Love and allow your heart and mind to be open to the Spirit of Love. It will set you free, heal and make whole those places in you that have been hurt by religion, man-made ideals, and human opinions. What matters is what God says about you, and He says you are fearfully and wonderfully made.

Congratulations JE...it's an honor to serve with you for such a time as this! I love you with all my heart!

Love NEVER Fails...

~ Debye Swilley

FAQs: THE BIG TEN

PREFACE

"One Thing I Can Tell You Is, You Got To Be Free"

They say that writers should write what they know.

Makes sense.

Well, OK then...here's what I know.

I know God.

I don't know everything about Him, but I know that He's real even though my perception of Him has changed rather profoundly over the course of my life and ministry, especially in the last few years.

I used to know everything about Him when I was a young preacher just starting out at the age of 13...when I was young, zealous, dynamic and committed...obsessively faithful to the call that I believed God had placed on my life. It was beautiful... you should have seen me. I was...how shall I put it?...oh, yeah... I was 'on fire for Jesus' and, quite frankly, completely arrogant and full of myself, in retrospect.

Well, maybe not completely arrogant...the touch of God on my life was real enough that it prevented my motives in ministry from being totally self-serving.

But, yes...definitely...back then I knew pretty much everything there was to know about God and the Bible and about what it meant to be a Christian.

Everything.

And I was happy to let you know that I knew everything, especially if you disagreed with what I believed was the truth. And if you disagreed with me, you were just dead wrong and that's all there was to it (which is why I can completely empathize now with many of my critics...but more about that later in the book).

Anyway, it's an awesome thing to know everything.

I just don't know where I lost that information.

Every now and then I'll drive by a church and will see written on their signage out front something like this: *"Our Mission: To Make Him Known to the World!"*

Sounds good.

Nice slogan.

But if you really think about it, it's a rather pretentious idea to assume that you know enough about God to make Him known to the whole world.

I know at this point (at least for myself) I can only tell you about the part of Him that I know (or know about)...about what I've learned on my journey...about how He's worked in my life...about what has worked for me in my spiritual evolution.

I can't and won't set myself up as someone who has such a grasp on the width and length and depth and height of the mysteries of God that I can tell you about Him fully. I now realize after many years of preaching (to be exact, 40 at the time of this writing), that I only see a little corner of the whole thing...the 'big picture' of God, if you will.

I know that I know in part and I prophesy in part.

The bottom line is, I'm only an authority on the subject of what I know about my relationship with Him.

Everyone else will have to work out their own salvation, including the ones who consider me to be their bishop/pastor teacher/spiritual leader. The sower simply sows the word... the different types of soil that receive the seed of it produce different results in their lives. If what I know and have learned (and continue to learn) about God can help another person on their own spiritual path, then, as the song says, my living shall not be in vain.

The other thing I know about is internal conflict...the kind of conflict that comes from living your life in a way that is contrary to your nature in order to conform to the appearance of what you believe...or of what you say you believe...or of what you think you believe...or of what you want to believe.

In a word, I know what it means to be gay in a world where being gay is unmentionable, unacceptable, damnable, abominable and just plain wrong...what it means to spend your entire life trying not to be something that you know you are, so as to support what you believe is right.

As I said, I used to know everything about God and the Bible (and if you don't realize that's a tongue-in-cheek statement, it's probably going to be a waste of your time trying to get through this book). But what I 'knew' and what I 'REALLY knew' were just totally incompatible.

I didn't grow up 'in the closet'; in the world in which I grew up, the closet would have been freedom. No, I wasn't in the closet; I was in a vault 100 feet underground where I refused to admit to myself on any level what I really knew to be true, because if I were to admit or accept that truth, I would have to reject the other truth...the Bible truth...the God truth. And that just couldn't be done.

I'll be saying a lot more about this in the following pages, but I want to establish first that, regardless of its sub-title, this isn't only a book about what it really means to be gay. It's a book about understanding in general...authenticity...the ability to be exactly *who* you are...exactly *how* you are...without any fear of being rejected by the God you believe in and about whom you preach.

Ultimately, then, it's really about GOOD NEWS.

I'll be discussing a lot of things about God and religion and spirituality and sexual orientation and about coming to terms with the truth that sets you free.

But before I explore any of that, I need to make a few statements of what I believe to be fact, and it's fine with me if you disagree with me; you certainly won't be the first. But you should know at the outset that this is what I believe to be true, and if you don't accept these statements, this book is only going to irritate you.

Anyway, here goes...

First, some people are gay, in the same way that some people are straight. There's a percentage of all people who are homosexual...about a tithe of the entire population by most estimates. The world isn't turning gay. No one can 'turn' gay... you either are or you aren't. No one can 'recruit' you to be either gay or straight.

Again, the world is not turning gay, even though many religious/conservative/fundamentalist people apparently seem to think that it is. There are no more gay people on the planet than there have ever been. It may appear that way, but that's because more people are free to talk about their sexual orientation now than in the past and because those people are more visible than they were before for any number of reasons.

People are who they are. Gay people aren't gay because they have sex with people of the same sex, in the same way that sex with the opposite sex doesn't make someone straight. In fact, there are gay people who have never had sex with the same sex, or sex at all for that matter...orientation is about orientation, not about activity.

There is no such thing as 'the gay lifestyle.'

Being gay is not a sexual fetish or an aberration.

It is not a choice. No one can choose homosexuality any more than they can choose heterosexuality.

If you are gay, you will always be gay, regardless of whether or not you have sex with the same sex or with the opposite sex or if you choose to be celibate.

I will say more about all of this but, before I do, I need to tell you that I already read the Bible. I need to establish that fact before anyone starts up their computer to send me a message from God.

I'm very familiar with the handful of passages that refer to homosexuality, which are, for the most part, a couple of statements made by Moses and a few others by Paul.

I am familiar with Leviticus, which I will later discuss.

And in the year prior to this writing, the first chapter of Romans and the sixth chapter of 1 Corinthians have been cut and pasted and sent to me about 2,500-3,000 times...so, even though I appreciate the fact that those who have sent me those passages have the ability to cut and paste with their computers, they should know that I have read, studied, meditated and wrestled my entire life and 40 years of ministry with said passages. The majority of my preaching is from Paul's epistles, so I'm pretty familiar with everything he said about everything.

Well, that's about it for opening statements. As I said, I'll come back to all of these things later in the book.

But for now, the most important thing I can tell you is that the Gospel is GOOD NEWS.

Period.

And at the end of the day, that's really what I want to talk about. But I have to get this other stuff out of the way first, so please bear with me if it's not applicable to you personally.

How am I going to bring all these topics together into one book that makes sense?

One chapter at a time.

So, let's get started.

CHAPTER ONE

"This Is My Story, This Is My Song"

*There is no greater agony
than bearing an untold story inside you.*
– Maya Angelou

Let's take it from the top.

I really want to talk about *you*.

Actually, I want to talk about God and you...about your relationship with Him.

I want to share the GOOD NEWS with you...

But first I need to tell you a little bit more about me so you'll understand where I'm coming from.

So, here goes...

There's certainly more to my life than this, but basically two profound realities concerning my identity as a human being exist...realities of which I have been fully aware for practically as long as I can remember.

These two absolutes have been the major part of everything I am, have influenced every decision I've ever made, and have shaped my particular and perhaps peculiar world-view throughout the entirety of my time on this planet.

Both things were, in my opinion, completely imposed upon me, as I didn't choose or ask for either one of them, and I came to realize early on that neither of them would ever go away.

But the thing that ultimately created what I always thought of as my 'impossible situation' was the fact that, as far as the world I came from (the one I already told you about) was concerned, these two aspects of my being were completely incompatible... incapable of the possibility of any compromise or co-existence.

The first absolute of which I speak is what I personally believe to be the call of God on my life.

I am a fourth-generation minister from the classical (legalistic/fundamentalist) Pentecostal tradition. My father and mother and both of my grandfathers were and are ministers from that same tradition; one of my great-grandfathers was a minister from an equally fundamentalist tradition and several (if not most) of my immediate relatives are also involved in ministry/church-work on some level, either full-time or part-time.

I certainly understand and appreciate my legacy and heritage, but my personal call was, I believe, unique to me and was not the result of any reluctant resignation on my part to join the family business.

Ministry and church are all that I have ever known, but my own experience with divine direction and God's anointing on my life is and has always been personally very real to me and I've never for a second doubted its validity.

At the time of writing this first chapter, I am 53 years old and am still, at least for now, the full-time Senior Pastor of the Charismatic megachurch (as I suppose it is still considered, according to church-growth definitions) that I founded right outside of metropolitan Atlanta, GA over 26 years ago.

For about half of that time I have been the Bishop over a network of churches and ministries around the United States, in the Philippines and in Uganda called NOW MINISTRIES, which is currently in transition for reasons that I will discuss later. Having begun preaching at the age of 13, I am now in my fortieth year of ministry.

I love God and, as I said previously, believe that He is real.

I was raised in the south (in the buckle of the Bible-belt) in old-school, old-time religion complete with hell-fire and brimstone and an absolute belief in an imminent end-of-the world apocalypse. I don't know if I can say that I really loved God as I was growing up, but I definitely feared Him. In fact, I was taught to fear God and the devil and hell and the possibility of losing my salvation and the possibility (if not probability) of missing "The Rapture" (see Glossary of Terms) and having to live through the "Great Tribulation" and the communists and pretty much everything else, as I remember it.

I also lived my whole life with another horrible fear, but I'll get to that in a minute.

The part about me being 'on fire for Jesus' that I was telling you about began a couple of months before my fourteenth birthday when I received what we in the Pentecostal church referred to as "The Baptism in the Holy Spirit." That night, I believed I heard God call me into the ministry, even though my parents tell me that I was actually preaching when I was in diapers.

Seriously.

Anyway, after that night I began preaching immediately at my high school and on street corners and in public parks and in prisons and hospitals and anywhere else a teenage kid could find an audience. I constantly did personal 'witnessing'... knocked on hundreds of doors to share the Gospel...passed out thousands of Gospel tracts. I can't even begin to count how many people I lead in "The Sinner's Prayer" during that period (which lasted for some years, by the way); I lead someone to Jesus nearly every day of my life back then. I was what we called a 'soul-winner' and I was good at it. (All of these words and phrases in quotation marks can be found in the Glossary of Terms for those of you who have no idea what I'm talking about.)

I was not just evangelical during that period...I was, in a word, obsessed.

I have my own thoughts about why I was so radically committed back then—hopefully some of the work I did during those years counted for something—but more than anything else, I believed that was what God required of me and I didn't want to disappoint or anger Him in any way. I guess I channeled a lot of my fear of God into trying to please Him by tirelessly working for Him that way...turning my childhood fear of hell-fire into a fiery teenage ministry that brought multitudes to a belief in Jesus Christ so that they wouldn't go to hell.

But the God that I believe in now is good and loving; in fact, I believe that He IS love.

Period.

I know He loves me, and I love Him back.

That's the GOOD NEWS I want to tell you about.

My theology has evolved over the years to a place of inclusion and tolerance/acceptance of other belief systems, but orthodox Christianity still holds my allegiance and maintains authority in my life.

I don't think that Jesus Christ is or ever would be as hostile and indifferent to people outside of Christianity as many of His 'followers' are, but I do believe that He is the crucified and risen Savior of the world.

I am persuaded that the Bible (although obviously subject to the fallibility of the humanity through which it was written) was and is ultimately inspired by the Holy Spirit.

I believe that prayer works.

I believe in miracles.

I believe in the Kingdom of God.

I believe that the Church is relevant to the world.

I believe that I am called.

> *For God's gifts and His call are irrevocable. [He never withdraws them when once they are given, and He does not change His mind about those to whom He gives His grace or to whom He sends His call.]*
> (Romans 11:29 – AMP)

"And Now For The Rest Of The Story . . ."

The other reality is my sexual orientation.

I am a gay man.

I've always been gay, even though I didn't know what to call it or how to explain it when I was a child.

I was born left-handed, but I was taught to live as a right-handed man in a predominately right-handed world. In the same way, I also believe that I was born gay and, even though there is no hard scientific proof yet that I am aware of to verify that, the fact is that I have had same-sex attraction for as long as I can remember; so whether or not I was actually born that way, my world-view was shaped as such so early on that I may as well have been.

This is an undisputed truth in my life, as far as I'm concerned, and yet I learned from a very early age that I had no choice but to live as a straight man in a predominately straight world, especially if I was going to be a Christian, much less a minister... and so I did.

The horrible fear that I mentioned above was the fear that if I were to let the important people in my life know about my orientation, they wouldn't love me any more.

Oh yeah, and the fear that if I admitted it I would go to hell...

...or be *"turned over to a reprobate mind"* (more about that later)...

I am a twice-divorced father of four wonderful kids (three sons, one daughter) and the grandfather to two little angels who are the light of my life. I will explore later in this writing why and how I was married and sired children (and, yes, they were conceived in the conventional way, if you must know).

I'm trying not to turn this into an autobiography...just got to tell you this part.

As I said in the Preface, it's a book about authenticity...about the power of learning to be yourself and about accepting the fact that God loves you just as you are.

I want to write something encouraging and empowering to those who have been bullied and beaten up by society or by the religious community because they are different or perceived to be different. The Bible shouldn't be used as a weapon and religion shouldn't be something that oppresses people.

The bottom line is that God loves you regardless of your gender, race, nationality, ethnicity, body-type, belief system or sexual orientation.

Really.

You're awesome in His sight simply because you are His creation.

> *Who in the world do you think you are to second-guess God? Do you for one moment suppose any of us knows enough to call God into question? Clay doesn't talk back to the fingers that mold it, saying, "Why did you shape me like this?"*
>
> (Romans 9:20 – The Message)

Anyway, to fast-forward the story and get to the incentive for writing this book, I finally 'came out' to the whole world on Wednesday, October 13, 2010.

I actually came out to Debye before we were married (but we got married anyway...more about that later), and I came out to my parents nearly a year before I did it publicly. I came out to my kids not long after that and then to my staff a little later, so October 13 of that year wasn't a shock for any of my immediate family or the people with whom I work.

But that night I shared something entitled, *"A Real Message to Real People"* with my congregation, which became the most watched/heard/talked about message of my entire years of ministry. In it I talked about these two realities...about my lifetime effort of trying to harmonize two personal absolutes which have been a part of me for as long as I can remember... one: the call of God on my life, the other: my sexual orientation.

I explained how I didn't ask for either of them and how through a series of events, including the amicable divorce that Debye had sought a year earlier, I had come to terms with both of them.

The tape of the service went viral on the internet almost immediately after I delivered the message, became for a few days the video with the most hits on YouTube, and garnered an unbelievable amount of unexpected media exposure in the following weeks and months.

The response to it was, for me, astounding.

On that Wednesday night I had no plan or outline of what I wanted to say...no script or pre-meditation of it at all. Had I known beforehand that the video was going to become so high profile, I would have no doubt phrased a few things that I said that night differently, but it was what it was.

But there was not one day in the following year that I didn't hear from someone somewhere in the world who wanted to thank me for it or tell me that it changed their perception of God or of religion or of people with same sex attraction.

Many told me that it changed or even saved their lives.

Atheists told me that it made them want to believe in God again.

Straight people told me it helped them come to terms with their gay friends and family members, or even with their own authenticity issues.

Some gay teens told me it kept them from considering suicide, and many of their parents told me that it opened up broken lines of communication and brought much-needed healing to their families.

So even though the letter of the message wasn't perfect, the spirit of it apparently came through loud and clear, and for that I am very grateful.

Anyway, there was a good bit of speculation at the time about my real reason for coming out when I did. On many of the

"Christian" blogs that discussed my coming out ad nauseam, the rumor was that there was a gay sex scandal about to come out on me and so I used the opportunity to get in front of the story and do some damage control; but that was not the case. No such scandal ever surfaced for the very simple reason that one did not exist.

No one outed me.

No one threatened to out me.

Even with Debye divorcing me, I could have gone the rest of my life and never publicly admitted to my sexuality; I could have just avoided the subject altogether, as many closeted celebrities and high profile ministers do.

Truth be told, if anything at all outed me (aside from an unprecedented number of gay teen suicides around that time) it was my own life's message of building the Kingdom of God with *Real People Experiencing the Real God in the Real World*©.

The truth really does make you free.

You know...authenticity.

GOOD NEWS.

Anyway, that's my story...most of it, at least.

I'll come back to a few things written in this chapter later.

OK, let's continue...

CHAPTER TWO

"I Want To Thank You For Lettin' Me Be Myself Again"

You're blessed when you're content with just who you are—no more, no less. That's the moment you find yourselves proud owners of everything that can't be bought.

(Matthew 5:5 – The Message)

"Line upon line...precept upon precept..."

That's a well-known Bible phrase that I like a lot.

To me it means that if you want to communicate effectively, you have to lay a foundation of what you want to say and then build upon it...and you have to build upon it, as that same Scripture goes on to say, *"here a little...there a little."*

I do have a lot of things that I want to communicate to you—many things I want to talk about here—but I need to lay a foundation first so that you can really understand with clarity my actual purpose in putting all of this out there.

As I said earlier, I'm just writing what I know and, most of all I know God, so my foundation has to be that of constructing somewhat of a theological framework. Otherwise, my subject matter becomes marginalized and trivialized.

Please don't let that be off-putting if you only picked up this book to read what I have to say about being gay.

It may sound like that part's going to be boring, but it's not. And it's important.

Everything I discuss will ultimately bring me back to the main topic of sharing the GOOD NEWS with you because, at the end of the day, that's really what I always want to talk about.

I was born to share GOOD NEWS.

The Spirit of the Lord God is upon me to do it.

I re-iterate: this isn't a 'gay' book. But I do think it's important that I deal with that whole subject from my God/Bible/Christian paradigm, and I will...everything from Sodom and Gomorrah to 'abominations' to what the Bible says about it (and doesn't say about it), to legalism and homophobia and so on.

I want to answer some of the questions on the topic that I'm asked pretty much all the time these days and discuss two of the most obnoxious phrases that I've ever heard (and, believe me, I've heard them a lot!).

They are:

God didn't make Adam and Steve; He made Adam and Eve!

and

Love the sinner, hate the sin!

I just really find both of those statements extremely offensive for different reasons, and I'll be happy to tell you why when I get to that part.

But I'm getting ahead of myself.

I'll get to it.

All in good time.

But my sexual orientation does not define me entirely.

After being in full-time ministry for the better part of half a century, I would like to be known and remembered for more than just being gay...or for being the gay Bishop...or the gay minister; I'm not denying or hiding (obviously) that part of me, but that's just one aspect of who I am.

But knowing both the God part and the gay part does put me in a position that makes me feel it's my responsibility to address sexual orientation from a God-perspective.

To whom much is given, much is required.

Bottom line, I'm going to tell you what I know about all that, but first I need to tell you what I know about this.

I think the easiest way to deal with my subject matter is to put it in question and answer form...to just give simple, straight-forward answers to the things that people ask me about the most.

So, for the sake of context, let me start here...

QUESTION #1: *Do you think your theology is 'orthodox'?*

ANSWER #1: *Yes, I do!*

Orthodoxy was a word that I rarely, if ever, heard while growing up in churches within the classical Pentecostal denominations. In that tradition, the emphasis was always placed upon the power and manifestation of the Holy Spirit, over and above the correctness of theology or Biblical doctrine.

Orthodoxy and all that it entails became a bigger part of my consciousness as I received my education, but it didn't really become so personally important to me until recent years.

The dictionary defines *orthodoxy* as the quality of being orthodox (especially in religion), a belief or orientation agreeing with conventional standards. The word is from the Greek *ortho* (right, correct) and *doxa* (thought, teaching, glorification) and is typically used to refer to the correct theological or doctrinal observance of religion as determined by some overseeing body; those beliefs which reflect the faith of the whole Church since the time of the apostles; a term used in a number of senses, of which the following are the most important: (1) Orthodoxy in the literal sense of 'right belief' as opposed to heresy; (2) Orthodoxy in the sense of the forms of Christianity which are dominant in the East.

As we examine the Apostles' Creed, the Nicene Creed and other historical and foundational Christian statements of faith, we see their relevance to ministry in the twenty-first century.

The more research I do, the more confirmation I receive that the message the world is really waiting for is organic, original and orthodox Christianity...the Gospel of the Kingdom, which is simply the GOOD NEWS.

No more.

No less.

The actual, original Gospel is preached so rarely these days in the mainstream churches, that when it is presented in a candid and uncomplicated manner, many people who think they are orthodox in their beliefs, actually believe that those who preach only the GOOD NEWS are unorthodox!

Amazing how things get turned around.

As far as I'm concerned, I don't think you can improve on what the angels announced to the shepherds in the Christmas story: *"Behold, I bring you GOOD NEWS of GREAT JOY which shall be to ALL PEOPLE...unto you is born this day a SAVIOR!"*

That's the Gospel, pure and simple.

GOOD NEWS.

GREAT JOY.

ALL PEOPLE.

In recent years I have particularly developed a greater appreciation for the Apostles' Creed, which is accepted by both the Roman Catholic and Protestant Church (the Greek Orthodox Church favors the nearly identical Nicene Creed) as an official confession of Christianity.

In both creeds (and this is true for all the other ancient Christian creeds) there is nothing mentioned about the devil, or a 'rapture' or a 'tribulation period' or Israel becoming a nation in 1948, or anything about hell and eternal damnation.

The older Roman Catholic version of the Apostles' Creed used to contain the phrase "He descended to hell," but the Modern English Version uses the more Biblically-accurate phrase: "He descended to the dead," because true Hebrew and Greek scholars can no longer deny that the Hebrew *sheol* and the Greek *Hades* should never have been interpreted as "hell," because they simply mean 'the grave' or, more specifically, 'the unseen.'

More about that a few pages later.

Anyway, here it is:

THE APOSTLES' CREED
(Modern English Version)

I believe in God, the Father Almighty,
Creator of heaven and earth.
I believe in Jesus Christ, God's only Son, our Lord,
Who was conceived by the Holy Spirit,
born of the Virgin Mary,
suffered under Pontius Pilate,
was crucified, died and was buried;
He descended to the dead.
On the third day He rose again;
He ascended to heaven,
He is seated at the right hand of the Father,
and He will come again to judge the living and the dead.
I believe in the Holy Spirit, the holy catholic church,
the communion of saints, the forgiveness of sins,
the resurrection of the body, and the life everlasting.
Amen.

This creed is basically what I believe and preach.

The only revision that I would make to it would be to replace the phrase "God's only Son" with "God's firstborn Son," because of Romans 8:29:

> *For those God foreknew he also predestined to be conformed to the image of his Son, that he might be the FIRSTBORN among many brothers and sisters.* (TNIV)

And I should also point out that the word *catholic* (lower case), simply means "the Church Universal, the Body of Christ."

This term is not to be confused with Roman Catholicism but is accepted by Roman Catholics and Protestants alike.

Webster defines *catholic* as "broad-minded, as in belief or tastes; liberal; comprehensive; large; universal in reach; general."

I love the Church of Jesus Christ with my whole heart, and I respect its ancient traditions. Jesus said He would build His church and that the gates of Hades (or the unseen) could not prevail against it. In other words, death or anything from the unseen realm (including the mysterious force of religion) cannot ever overpower the life-giving power of the Gospel of Jesus Christ, the Word made flesh, Who was crucified, buried and resurrected and is the Head of the Church, the Lord of the Universe and the Savior of all people, especially those who believe.

So, the answer to the question about my theology is, yes, I most definitely do believe that it's orthodox.

Next question...

CHAPTER THREE

"Jesus Is Just Alright With Me"

*We can set no limits to the agency of the Redeemer
to redeem, to rescue, to discipline in his work,
and so will he continue to operate after this life.*
– Clement of Alexandria (c.150-211/216)

I've actually had two public 'coming out' experiences.

The one that I discussed a couple of chapters ago was my second.

The first one happened a few years ago when I finally came out doctrinally, if you will, and started preaching with confidence what I had been seeing in the Scriptures for some time about Jesus being the Savior of the whole world.

At that time words and labels like

Inclusion,

Ultimate Reconciliation,

Universalism,

Christian Universalism, etc. began to be associated with and ascribed to me,

I suppose I shouldn't bring up something negative in a book that's about GOOD NEWS (come to think of it, I've already brought up some negative things, so I guess it's no big deal to add one more), but in many ways this first coming out seemed to be more controversial than the second one!

I've witnessed two rather significant exoduses (exodi?) of people from my church...the most obvious one—the one I've become most known for—was the result of telling the people who I really *am*...the other (previous) one—the one that didn't get picked up by the media—was the result of my telling the people what I really *believe.*

Truth be told, I'm pretty sure more people disconnected themselves from me and my ministry over my saying that the work of Jesus (the Last Adam) completely trumped the work of the first Adam, than left me because I admitted I was gay.

The biggest issue for everyone in that first exodus was over my challenging the conventional religious ideas about hell and eternal punishment.

In general, it's really important to a lot of people, especially Christians it seems, that someone somewhere burns in hell for eternity.

And here's what's especially interesting/funny/ironic to me about all that: when I came out about my sexual orientation, nearly every ministry that had ever networked with me on any level over the years instantly and completely severed all ties with me. In that first year it was like I went through a thousand little divorces from people who had been like family to me; some of them had been in my life for 30 years or more and they immediately cut me off, entirely.

So I had to look for new people to connect with...you just can't be out there all alone...

Well, as it turns out, there are actually a lot of gay or gay-friendly or gay-affirming ministries all over the place (if you know where to look) and I've been received by a few of them; some of them have even invited me to preach in their churches.

But when people ask me if I've been welcomed by the gay community since coming out, the answer is yes and no...and mostly no when it comes to gay religious people.

There's a huge part of that population that has been so brutalized, rejected and hurt by the Church that they've just turned their back on the idea of God altogether.

Pretty much every message or piece of mail that I've received from those who fall into that category has been beautiful, supportive, touching, and effusive with thanks and praise for everything I've said publicly about God and gays.

In a word, those people love me.

A lot.

But they don't go to church or support ministries, so basically they have said a very nice 'thank you' and then have gone back to the safety of their atheism, agnosticism and/or private and personal spirituality. A minister...any minister (even a gay one)...just represents too much pain and heartache to them because of their own histories.

And so my reception by them has been marginal, at best.

There's another part of the religious gay community that is very connected to the formal, more liturgical churches. They, for the most part, have been warm and cordial to me, but they generally don't know how to relate to my kind of preaching or the Charismatic worship style of my two congregations, so they keep their distance.

Then there are the gay evangelical or Pentecostal or Spirit-filled or Full-Gospel ministries that would typically be more similar or friendlier to my type of ministry.

They're very nice.

But I discovered quickly that my theology of the finished work of the cross is considered too 'out there'...too edgy...for many if not most of them.

In other words, 'affirming' churches are not, as a rule, 'inclusive.'

Go figure.

In fact, many of them consider inclusion to be a false doctrine, and my teaching of eternal punishment (or lack, thereof) is a deal breaker for pretty much all of them.

So, suffice it to say, I have had to learn to be content in isolation.

The people from my 'Egypt' have nothing to do with me now, but neither do a lot of the people in my 'Canaan,' if that makes sense.

Jesus went to the wilderness after His baptism.

Paul went to Arabia after his conversion.

John was exiled to the Isle of Patmos because of His revelation.

I just told the truth about all of me, including about what I believe, and the truth set me free from most relationships.

My wilderness was psychological.

Straight church people are generally incredulous when I tell them that I can't preach in most gay churches that I've encountered because they very strongly believe in The Rapture and the Great Tribulation and most certainly in a literal, burning hell reserved for unbelievers, and they consider me to be errant in my theology of ultimate grace.

Straight church people can't believe that I'm considered too liberal for gay church!

I guess on some level they must believe, at least sub-consciously, that gay people are, in fact, going to hell themselves and are shocked to find out that hell is such a big part of the belief-system of a lot of Christian gay people.

I must say, I was a little surprised by it myself.

But I gave up trying to make sense of religion a long time ago, so it is what it is.

"Oh, How I Love Jesus"

Anyway, as I've already stated, I was raised with the scary, judgmental, *"coming as a thief in the night,"* all-seeing-eye, holiness-demanding, intolerant Jesus who was coming any minute to separate the sheep from the goats (and most of the people on the earth, I was taught, were hell-bound goats!).

Then when I started in the ministry myself (my 'on fire for Jesus' phase), I began to preach a more positive message of a loving Jesus with a New Testament emphasis on grace.

But back then I still believed that most people would probably not accept Jesus as their Savior and would therefore miss The Rapture and most likely end up in hell.

So I preached a lot of mercy and grace, but I also preached about the wrath of God for those who rejected that mercy and grace. That's what I was taught to believe and not question, even though it never felt right to me in my spirit.

Never could really accept the fact that a loving God could send people into eternal punishment.

And the more I got into studying the New Testament and original Bible languages and church history, it made less and less sense to me.

In the early days I was much more interested in 'souls' than I was in people, which is why I said in the Preface that I was so full of myself back then. I was an effective 'soul-winner' because it made me feel good about myself to think I was keeping people out of hell by my preaching.

I said the ministry was about helping others, but it was really about helping me...about how it made me feel about myself. That feeling of elation that comes from believing you're pleasing God by ministering in that way helps diffuse any feelings of self-loathing you may have about your very hidden sexual orientation.

In other words, once I realized that I couldn't pray the gay away (and I realized that early on), I just immersed myself in the kind of ministry that I thought most pleased God.

It may sound crazy, but the thought pattern goes something like this: If I can make God see me as a great soul-winner, maybe He won't notice that I'm really gay. Homosexuals are repulsive to God, but soul winners are really important to Him...exalted, even...they get special crowns in heaven for the amount of people they've brought with them...sort of like an eternal perk... like receiving a spiritual finder's fee...homosexuals, on the other hand, are fried forever in the flames...so...you do the math...

I became a soul-winner.

I'm not saying that's the only reason...the only motivation, but it's a big part of it.

That may be too real for some people.

Maybe I'm being too transparent.

But at this point I have nothing to hide, so I might as well tell it all.

So what does that have to do with Jesus?

Just this: after all is said and done—and even though I've come full-circle with it all—I still really do believe in and love Jesus with a pure heart and believe in what He did on the cross and in His resurrection, now more than ever.

Here are the two questions that I've been asked the most since I came out, theologically.

QUESTION #2: *Do you believe that Jesus Christ is the only way to God?*

ANSWER #2*: Undoubtedly!*

It is written in the Scriptures:

> *He is the Savior of ALL people, especially those who believe: This is why we've thrown ourselves into this venture so totally. We're banking on the living God, SAVIOR OF ALL MEN AND WOMEN, ESPECIALLY BELIEVERS.*
>
> (1 Timothy 4:10 – The Message)

The main purpose of the ministry is to declare the evangel, or the GOOD NEWS, that the Lamb of God has taken away the sin of the whole world.

He has saved everyone, but not everyone knows or believes it yet (and there is definitely an advantage to being one of the ones who *"especially believes"*...it's the way into the Kingdom!).

But in the same way that the Prodigal Son was always a son, even though he was lost and living in a pig sty, all of humanity is in the family of God (Ephesians 3:14, 15) but most of them are lost and living in their own 'pig sties' of religion, unbelief, deception or bondage.

They're just away from home *("All we like sheep have gone astray...").*

They need to hear the Word of Reconciliation so that they can "come to themselves" as did the Prodigal Son and then come back to the Father of us all.

That's why in John 14:6 we hear Jesus say so confidently:

> *I am the Way, the Truth, and the Life,*
> *and NO ONE comes to the Father except by Me!*

He had already declared in Chapter 12 that if He was lifted up from the earth on the cross, He would draw (literally the Greek uses the word "drag") ALL people to Himself.

The work that Jesus did on that cross for all of us is universal, unparalleled and unrivaled; the cross is the nexus (the thing that brings everything together) of the universe!

I don't believe that Jesus Christ is competitive with or hostile and antagonistic to

Buddha,

Muhammad,

Moses,

Confucius,

and others of that group...

Jesus told His disciples that *"whoever is not against us is for us."*

But because His atoning sacrifice and resurrection sets Him above and apart from every other sage, prophet, messiah or spiritual/religious leader in history, I still believe in His unique superiority.

All of the others were great seers and teachers and should be honored for their contribution to the world, but Jesus Christ alone is the *Savior* of the world.

In a word, Jesus Christ is Lord.

There.

I said it.

My knees bow and my tongue confesses to the glory of God that Jesus Christ is Lord.

But even though I believe that Jesus is ultimately the one way to God, I do not believe that all the

Jews,

Muslims,

Buddhists,

Hindus,

Sikhs,

Hare Krishnas,

agnostics and atheists, etc.

are all going to eventually walk down the aisle of a Christian church and pray "The Sinner's Prayer" and confess Romans 10:9 and 10.

Nor do I believe that they are damned and going to a place called hell if they don't (I promise I'll get to the hell subject shortly...).

Let me explain.

Quite simply, Jesus of Nazareth perfectly embodied and manifested what we call "the Christ" and it's Christ that is actually the way to God.

Jesus was and is the Christ, but the Christ was here before Jesus was born in Bethlehem.

According to Paul, centuries before Jesus' Incarnation, even Israel in the wilderness was "in Christ":

> *For I do not want you to be ignorant of the fact, brothers and sisters, that our ancestors were all under the cloud and that they all passed through the sea. They were all baptized into Moses in the cloud and in the sea. They all ate the same spiritual food and drank the same spiritual drink; for they drank from the spiritual rock that accompanied them, AND THAT ROCK WAS CHRIST.*
>
> (1 Corinthians 10:1-4 – TNIV)

And the writer of Hebrews said that Moses, while growing up in polytheistic Egypt, definitely knew "Christ" even though he would have no way of knowing who Jesus was:

> *By faith Moses, when he had grown up, refused to be known as the son of Pharaoh's daughter. He chose to be mistreated along with the people of God rather than to enjoy the fleeting pleasures of sin. He regarded disgrace FOR THE SAKE OF CHRIST as of greater value than the treasures of Egypt, because he was looking ahead to his reward.*
>
> (Hebrews 11:24-26 – TNIV)

That's why I always say there are those who *know His name,* but *don't know Him,* just as there are those who *know Him,* even though they don't *know His name.*

In my belief system, there is definitely one way to God and that is Christ...and flesh and blood cannot reveal Christ to us.

One way to God.

Many ways to Christ...

And Jesus is the Christ, but it is Christ, not Christianity, that is the way, the truth and the life.

So, yes...undoubtedly, I believe that Jesus Christ is the Way!

And here's the other most-asked question...

QUESTION #3: *Do you believe one must confess the Lordship of Jesus Christ to be saved?*

ANSWER #3: *Absolutely!*

But it's really an unnecessary question (a moot point, if you will) in that it has already been answered in the Scriptures... it is written that every knee WILL bow and every tongue WILL confess that Jesus Christ is Lord, either now or later, to the glory of God the Father!

> *Therefore [because He stooped so low] God has highly exalted Him and has freely bestowed on Him the name that is above every name, that in (at) the name of Jesus every knee should (must) bow, in heaven and on earth and under the earth, and every tongue [frankly and openly] confess and acknowledge that Jesus Christ is Lord, to the glory of God the Father.*
> (Philippians 2:9-11 – AMP)

What is the official Christian method or formula for obtaining salvation?

It depends on whom you ask.

Some say that it is water baptism by immersion...

others say that it is baptism by sprinkling,

still others by christening/infant Baptism,

or baptism in the name of Jesus,

or baptism by invoking the Father, Son and Holy Spirit,

or Holy Spirit Baptism with the evidence of Speaking with Other Tongues,

or 'calling on The Name,'

or catechism,

or receiving Last Rites,

or by church membership,

or by repentance from dead works,

or by sanctification and holy living,

or by public confession...the list goes on and on.

In the Gospels, Zacchaeus received salvation simply by restoring, fourfold, all that he had stolen from the people (without baptism or confession of faith)...

The harlot received salvation simply by washing Jesus' feet with her hair (without baptism or confession of faith)...

The thief on the cross received salvation by simply asking for it (without baptism or confession of faith).

Paul and Silas told their believing jailer that his entire household would be saved just because they were related to him.

According to the Apostle Paul, all of humanity was 'saved' at the same time (1 Timothy 4:10), but all are not yet believers.

He also emphatically answered this often-asked question: "Does one have to confess the Lordship of Jesus to be eternally saved?" with a definite Yes!

He said that every tongue in heaven or on earth or "beneath the earth," according to His revelation of grace, should, and eventually will, confess...either now or later!

Absolutely, everyone must confess the Lordship of Jesus Christ to be saved and, thank God, according to the Scriptures, eventually everyone will!

One Other Thought...

It was suggested by someone (maybe more than one person, actually) that over the last few years I 'created' a theology for myself that would make it easier for me to come out as a gay man; in other words, I just did away with hell entirely so that I could say I was gay with no fear of being sent to that bad place where all the gays go, according to conventional church-wisdom.

When I first heard this accusation, I deeply resented it because what I believe about the Scriptures and about Jesus (the Word made flesh) is the result of years and years of my own prayer and study and revelation.

Preaching the Ministry of Reconciliation—the saving of the whole world by Jesus Christ on the cross—is not a theological fad for me.

I don't believe in it because someone else taught it or because it's a popular teaching (because it's not...).

I am not a devotee of any other preacher or teacher; what I believe and preach is what I really and deeply believe to be true.

But the more I thought about it, the more I realized that the accusation may not be entirely untrue, and I came to terms with it.

I can say that with no apology.

As I already said, I'm left-handed...I was born that way. I know I didn't choose it, but there was a time in history (and not really that long ago) that left-handed people were burned at the stake by the Church because they were thought to be demon-possessed.

Had I lived in that time, I'm sure my left-handedness would have forced me into a deeper study of the Scriptures...that is, if I had time when I wasn't running for my life!

I'm sure I would have thought that God just couldn't be so impossibly unfair as to create you as you are but then send you to hell because of the very way He created you!

And even though the right-handed people couldn't understand why some people 'chose' the evil left-handed lifestyle, I would want to make them understand that even if left-handed people forced themselves to write with their right hands to please God, by nature they were still and always would be left-handed. They could write with their right hands, but it would always feel wrong (unnatural) to them.

I have blue eyes, but if I had read in the Bible that all blue-eyed people go to hell, I think it's safe to say that I could not have accepted that. My biological reality, together with my belief in God, would force me into a deeper study of the Scriptures... because if God's that mean and unjust, then we're all in big trouble.

So, did my being gay force me into being open to interpreting the Scriptures differently than in the way I had been taught about salvation and grace and eternity and all that?

Perhaps.

Probably.

But if that's what it took to move me into a discovery of the fullness of the Truth, then so be it.

I would hope that I would have come to my theological conclusions had I been born heterosexual, but who knows?

One way or the other, it's all good.

It has brought me to the conclusion that, in the big picture, all that really matters is the GOOD NEWS.

OK, enough about that...I have other questions to answer...

But, yes, Jesus is the way...

Jesus is Lord.

CHAPTER FOUR

"Don't Worry, Be Happy"

Summing it all up, friends, I'd say you'll do best by filling your minds and meditating on things true, noble, reputable, authentic, compelling, gracious— the best, not the worst; the beautiful, not the ugly; things to praise, not things to curse. Put into practice what you learned from me, what you heard and saw and realized. Do that, and God, who makes everything work together, will work you into his most excellent harmonies.

(Philippians 4:8, 9 – The Message)

It's better to be positive than to be negative.

Don't you think so?

The Gospel...the GOOD NEWS...is, and should be, nothing but a completely positive message.

When the angels appeared to the shepherds in the Christmas story, they didn't ask them, *"If you died tonight, do you know where you would spend eternity?"*

They simply announced the GOOD NEWS to them.

GOOD NEWS to ALL PEOPLE.

Period.

On the Day of Pentecost, the diverse population of Jerusalem heard nothing but a positive message delivered in Spirit-speak by the 120 who had been in the Upper Room.

They responded to them by saying, *"Do we not hear them speaking (only) the wonderful works of God in our own languages?"*

Jesus said that the Gospel was proactive, consisting of two Do's as opposed to the ten Don'ts that Moses received on Mt. Sinai. In the New Covenant, *thou shalt not* is replaced with (you SHALL) *"love the Lord your God with all your heart* and (you SHALL) *"love your neighbor as yourself."*

That's all the Gospel is.

Just two things.

Love God.

Love others.

To make it out to be anything more than that is, in my opinion, antichrist.

It's why the cross...something made of only two simple beams, a vertical and a horizontal...is the symbol of Christianity.

Two beams.

Two commandments.

That's all.

Even though it's been used as an image of hate in some instances—been burned on some front lawns as an intimidation tactic by some messed up people, etc.—it's still the perfect symbol for the simplicity that is in Christ.

When Jesus appeared to people, both before and after His resurrection, His first words to them were nearly always, *"Fear not!"*

The GOOD NEWS should always confirm that salutation.

Kind of makes you wonder how the message of Christianity turned into one that is so fear-based.

"Come Fly With Me"

And speaking of fear...

I've already mentioned "The Rapture" several times in this book (don't try to look it up in a concordance because the word's not in the Bible), but if you weren't raised with the awareness of it looming over every day of your life—didn't have it as a main factor in every decision you made...if you never lived with the constant dread of it possibly occurring at any minute and the fear that it most likely would be occurring without you being a part of it because you weren't good enough...or holy enough—then you can't appreciate what it can do to a person.

Fear really messes with your mind, especially when it's ever-present. Seriously, if you weren't raised with the daily threat that He was coming *"as a thief in the night,"* you can't imagine what it was like for those of us who were.

You never rest well when you're afraid you may be the victim of a robbery.

OK, so anyway, I knew I had same-sex attraction as early as age four...don't ask me how I knew, I just did. And most of the gay people who write to me to tell their horror stories of failed exorcisms, conversion therapies, shock treatments, ex-gay programs and other such nonsense, tell me that they knew at or around that age, too. Amazing how so many preschoolers were able to 'choose the gay lifestyle' even before they learned how to ride a bike!

But I digress.

Point being, one main reason I never considered either the probability or the necessity of my coming out—why I never thought my orientation was ever going to be a big deal in my life—is that I was raised believing that the end of the world was imminent.

I realized early on that my psychological wiring wasn't the work of a demon...wasn't a phase...or a sickness...or a mental illness. It certainly wasn't a choice (more about that later). So, I accepted the fact that it wasn't going to change and that I was in an impossible situation because of it and because of my call to the ministry, as I've already stated.

Any gay Christian who grew up knowing at least a little bit about the Bible probably has identified at some point with Paul talking about his mysterious *"thorn in the flesh"* that God refused to remove from him, even though he prayed three   times that He would. Well, some of us prayed three thousand, maybe three *million* times that our "thorn" would be removed, but ultimately we had to settle for believing that His grace would be sufficient to help us manage it.

But the reason I could deal with my own thorny reality is because I thought, for the majority of my young life, that I would be flying away at any minute and then I would go to heaven where Jesus could fix me. Don't get me wrong, The Rapture was never something I looked forward to. The thought of it always scared me and made me very sad at the prospect of it preventing me from living out my life on the earth. But at least, I thought, it would take care of the problem.

Then, over the years as my theology progressed and evolved and I came to believe that the Bible didn't really support John Nelson Darby's (the father of 'The Rapture') teaching, I just immersed myself more and more into the ministry. I dated girls and eventually got married with the intention of finally changing myself into a heterosexual...or at least learning to act like one. I mean, how hard could it be, really? If you believe the trumpet could be sounding at any minute, you at least know your condition of trying to be something you're not is at the very least temporary and, therefore, doable and bearable.

Anyway, back to my point about being positive.

I have no regrets now about anything in my spiritual/ theological journey, including my life with The Rapture.

It was what it was.

Growing up, I heard nearly every week in church that He was coming for those *"who love His appearing"* (which always worried me because I didn't really love it like I thought I should).

But I do love it now.

Now that phrase means something quite different to me, and I do love His appearing every day of my life with every new revelation of Him...every epiphany...every time I go from glory to glory and find Him in every one of those incarnations.

The Daystar has risen in my heart.

It's why, I believe, that Jesus said *"no man knows the day or the hour"* of His appearing...it's because it's not a single event...it happens at different times and it happens differently for every person.

Nowadays, if and when people ask me if I don't believe in The Rapture any more, I refuse to answer that question.

Well, it's not that I refuse to answer so much as I try to re-direct the framework of the conversation.

I don't ever want to be known as someone who *doesn't* believe in something.

I don't want to be known for *not* believing in The Rapture or for *not* believing in hell.

I want to be known for what I (do) believe!

If Darby was right and there is, indeed, a Rapture...if I literally hear Gabriel blow his heavenly horn...I promise you that I'll fly away with you and the other believers to wherever they're/ we're going to go for seven years before re-entering the earth's atmosphere, and I will deliver a sincere apology to all concerned for getting it so wrong.

In the meantime, here's what I've been saying for years, and anyone who has any depth of understanding at all about these things will know what I mean by it. I'm going to use some terminology here that may be completely foreign to you.

If it is, don't worry about it.

It doesn't really matter anyway.

QUESTION #4: *Do you believe in The Rapture of the Church?*

ANSWER #4: *Yes, I believe in a Pre-Tribulation Rapture of the Church.*

If that doesn't happen,

I believe in a Mid-Tribulation Rapture of the Church.
If that doesn't happen,

I believe in a Post-Tribulation Rapture of the Church.

If that doesn't happen,

I believe that Jesus Christ will come back to the earth through the clouds in bodily form.

If THAT doesn't happen,

I believe that there will eventually be a global, cosmic paradigm shift where the entire population of the earth will finally see the Christ...a time when His Spirit is poured out on all humanity, and "every eye shall see Him!"

Bottom line, it's all good.

Really.

All kidding aside, if you believe we're in the last days, it's fine with me.

Namaste.

If you believe in The Rapture, cool.

If you're really looking forward to it, far be it from me to take away your hope.

Go ahead and believe.

All things are possible.

As I said, if there is one, I'm flying, too.

If I'm wrong about it all, you can sit next to me at "the Marriage Supper of the Lamb" and say, "I told you so."

Just promise me you won't forget the part about the GOOD NEWS in whatever you believe.

It's very important.

CHAPTER FIVE

"No Hell Below Us, Above Us Only Sky"

SCARLETT: *Oh, Rhett. I am so afraid.*
RHETT: *I don't believe it. You've never been afraid in your life.*
SCARLETT: *I'm afraid now. I'm afraid of dying, of going to Hell.*
RHETT: *You look pretty healthy. And maybe there isn't any Hell.*
SCARLETT: *Oh, there is. I know there is. I was raised on it.*
– Gone With The Wind

As far as I recall, in the 40 years that I have been in the ministry, no one has ever one time asked me if I preach the Cross of Jesus Christ.

No one has asked if I pray for people to be filled with the Holy Spirit.

No one has ever asked if I feed the poor...

...or visit people in prison.

No one has inquired about my role in racial reconciliation,

or showed any curiosity, whatsoever, about whether or not I do anything to help the homeless...

...or drug addicts

...or alcoholics.

It has never even once come up in conversation and no one has even thought to ask if I preach on love and forgiveness...at least not that I can remember at the moment.

In fact, as I write this, I don't even remember if anyone has ever asked if I believe in a literal heaven with streets of gold and gates of pearl.

But people have always asked me lots and lots and lots of questions about hell, especially in the last few years...

"Do you believe in hell?"

"Do you believe in the fire and the brimstone?"

"Who do you think is going to hell?"

"When are they going to go?"

"Will they start burning as soon as they die?"

"How long will they burn?"

"Are there degrees of punishment in hell?"

"Who is in hell now?"

"Do people feel the fire scorching and burning their flesh for ever and ever and ever there?"

"Do the demons torture you in hell?"

"Are all the Jews and Muslims and atheists and homosexuals going to hell?"

...and so it goes.

I can even say something about heaven possibly being just another dimension and no one will bat an eye. But when you mess with the conventional religious ideas about hell that exist in peoples' heads, you stir up a lot of stuff and you find out how obsessed with it, and even defensive for it, many of them can be (and are).

In the last several years I've taught extensively on this subject and have examined, in-depth, the four words that were translated into "hell" in the King James Version and in some other translations.

I've explained that the word **Sheol** was simply the Hebrew word for 'the grave' or 'the unseen,' even though it was translated as "hell" in the Old Testament...look it up;

...that **Gehenna** (or the Valley of Hinnom) that Jesus referred to was in reality a literal, burning garbage dump right outside the city of Jerusalem...a very nasty place, indeed (I've been there and it's actually quite nice now, especially since they stopped sacrificing babies to the god Molech there...a well-kept grassy area at the foot of the Mount of Olives). But when Jesus discussed Gehenna in His teachings (the word that Bible interpreters centuries later decided to call "hell"), His audience had no concept of a fiery place of eternal punishment at the center of the earth...maybe because they would have assumed then that the earth was flat...or maybe because He was pointing to the geographical location of Gehenna when He referred to it (it's literally right outside the wall of the Old City of Jerusalem). But, whatever the case, the Jews didn't preach eternal punishment, so it would have never entered their minds that that was what He was talking about in the Sermon on the Mount...maybe because that was NOT what He was talking about!

...that **Tartarus** was a place of confinement for rebellious angels until the reconciliation of all things;

...and that **Hades** (a word that Jesus only used twice) is the name of the pagan god of the underworld in Greek mythology and was used as the Greek equivalent of the Hebrew *Sheol.*

I've also made mention of the fact that "hell" was never once mentioned in the original (Hebrew) language of the Old Testament. A place of eternal punishment is nowhere to be found in the OT. Adam and Eve were told they would *die* for transgressing the commandment of God...not go to a place called hell. Moses said that those who violated the Ten Commandments would be *executed*...not go to a place called hell. The inhabitants of the cities that were destroyed by fire only experienced a physical death...they were never threatened with a place of eternal punishment.

David actually said *"If I make my bed in **the grave** (not in "hell"* as it reads in some translations), *behold You are there";* he also said, *"You will not leave my soul **in the grave**..."* (not in "hell" as many people teach today).

David never heard of hell.

Nor did Abraham or Moses or Elijah or Isaiah or any of the other prophets; the concept of a place of eternal punishment was borrowed from other religions and inserted into Christianity some centuries after Jesus walked the earth.

There is no hell mentioned anywhere in any of Paul's Epistles.

Really.

John's prophetic vision of a "Lake of Fire" in The Revelation was from the Greek word *pur* and was symbolic of God's purifying fire (same root as *"baptized with the Holy Spirit and fire"* or *"our God is a consuming fire"* – KJV). I've even written about and spoken on the topic of "The Second Death" or when Hades ("hell" in the KJV) is thrown into the Lake of Fire (Revelation 20:14) and how it literally refers simply to "the death of death," proving that "hell" and the "Lake of Fire" are two completely different things.

That being said, and in spite of all that I've expressed, the point of our theology should never be about disproving the existence of a literal "hell" or a place of eternal punishment and damnation for the wicked or unsaved.

As I said in the previous chapter, I never want to be known for not believing in something.

The main theme and constant of everything that we study and believe should always be the complete triumph of the Lamb of God!

You know...the GOOD NEWS!

In other words, if there were a thousand literal, eternally burning hells, the redeeming power of the Lamb's ultimate and bloody sacrifice on the cross, His miraculous resurrection and His subsequent intercession for all of humanity (Hebrews 7:25) would still be a stronger force than all the combined hells that anyone could *imagine!*

That's why we behold the *Lamb* who takes away the sin of the world; it's not about what we don't believe in, it's about in what—or rather in Whom—we believe!

And because we believe in Him, we behold *Him* (not the absence of hell or the presumed liberty or imagined sins of others), and because we behold Him, we worship Him in Spirit and in truth!

So here's the big question...

QUESTION #5: *Do You believe in a literal hell?*

ANSWER #5: *Here's what I BELIEVE IN...*

I BELIEVE in the living God Who is the Savior of all men, especially of those who believe (1 Timothy 4:10), and that His salvation will ultimately reconcile all of humanity to Himself...

I BELIEVE that Jesus Christ is the Lamb slain from the foundation of the world (Revelation 13:8), and I believe in beholding the Lamb of God who takes away the sin of the world (John 1:29)...

I BELIEVE that every knee in heaven and on earth and under the earth will eventually bow and that every tongue in heaven and on earth and under the earth will eventually confess to the glory of God that Jesus Christ is Lord (Philippians 2:9, 10)...

I BELIEVE that all were condemned in Adam, but all are justified in Christ (Romans 5:17-21), for as in Adam all die, even so in Christ shall all be made alive (1 Corinthians 15:22), so I BELIEVE we were lost in Adam, but found in Christ...condemned in Adam, but justified in Christ...dead in Adam, but alive in Christ...

I BELIEVE that Jesus Christ was and is the atoning sacrifice for our sins, and not for our sins only, but also for the sins of the whole world (1 John 2:22)...

I BELIEVE that He has removed our transgressions from us as far as the east is from the west (Psalm 103:12)...

I BELIEVE we were chosen in Him before the foundation of the world, that we should be holy and without blame before Him in love (Ephesians 1:4)...

I BELIEVE that, because Jesus was lifted up from the earth on the cross, He will ultimately draw (the Greek uses the word "drag") all peoples unto Himself (John 12:32), *but that we can all still come to Him of our own free will...*

I BELIEVE that the glory of the Lord shall be revealed, and all humanity shall see it together (Isaiah 40:5)...

I BELIEVE that He will pour out of His Spirit on all humanity (Joel 2:28)...

I BELIEVE that every eye shall see Him (Revelation 1:7)...

I BELIEVE that it is not His will that any should perish (2 Peter 3:9)...

I BELIEVE that the grace of God that brings salvation has appeared to all people (Titus 2:11)...

I BELIEVE that God was in Christ, reconciling the world unto Himself, not imputing their trespasses to them (2 Corinthians 5:19)...

I BELIEVE that God has not appointed us unto wrath, but to obtain salvation by our Lord Jesus Christ (1 Thessalonians 5:9)...

I BELIEVE that we will not all sleep in death, but we shall all be changed (1 Corinthians 15:51)...

I BELIEVE that all things shall be made subject to Him so that God may be all in all (1 Corinthians 15:28)...

I BELIEVE that Christ is all and is in all (Colossians 3:11).

I know that's a long answer...I actually could have made it a lot longer...but I think you get the point.

Bottom line, I'm not trying to disprove the existence of hell to anyone...I just want everyone to know the GOOD NEWS.

God wins.

Love wins.

God is love.

God loves you as you are because He made you as you are.

Last Adam trumps first Adam.

Jesus wasn't delusional when He said on the cross, *"It is finished!"*

It really was.

And is.

Wow...now, that's GOOD NEWS!

CHAPTER SIX

"Bad Boys, Bad Boys, Whatcha Gonna Do?"

The evil that men do lives after them;
the good is oft interred with their bones.
– William Shakespeare

Morality matters.

Sin is a bad idea.

Of course, the definition of morality is different for every person, and after Jesus preached the Sermon on the Mount, pretty much everything was labeled by Him as a sin.

According to His startling revelation that day (*"You have heard it said, but I SAY..."*), if you hate your brother, you are a murderer; if you fantasize about committing adultery, it's exactly the same thing as actually going through with it; if you call your brother *raca* (the equivalent of calling him a faggot), you should be brought before the Council; and if you call him a fool, you are in danger of the fires of Gehenna (traditionalists say hell). Also, if you commit any of these type sins, you should dismember yourself (*"If your hand offends you, cut it off...if your eye offends you, gouge it out"...*).

And you thought Moses was hard.

Of course, Jesus' intention in this sermon was to show the futility of the Law and to leave us no alternative but to lose ourselves in His righteousness...to recognize that we are crucified and risen with Him...to reckon ourselves to be "IN CHRIST" so that we could return to God's original desire for His creation to walk in a *"Tree of Life"* paradigm as opposed to that of the *"Tree of the Knowledge of Good and Evil."*

Still, the Scriptures say that *the wages of sin is death.*

...that *the way of the transgressor is hard.*

...that *they who sow to the flesh will of the flesh reap corruption.*

So, morality...good.

Immorality...bad.

And righteousness, holiness, uprightness...however you may define them...are things to which you should aspire.

And integrity is important.

And character, goodness, virtue, ethics, principles and standards are all desirable things.

And criminals should pay their debt to society.

And people should be held responsible for their actions.

And you should always try to do the right thing, even when other people don't.

To me, saying all this is stating the obvious, but there are those who apparently think that when you preach the triumph of the cross over sin or the restitution of all things...when you proclaim that the Lamb of God took away the sin of the world...you are somehow giving license to people to live reckless, immoral, undisciplined, ungodly lives with no repercussions for the bad things they may do.

I mean...why not? You have told them that in the end they will all be reconciled to God no matter what, because of what Jesus did on the cross, so it's not about their righteousness anyway, right? Their righteousness is *"as filthy rags"* and therefore they shouldn't even bother with pointless attempts at discipline or self-control... shouldn't waste their time trying to live a holy or moral existence at all. Everyone is in Christ, so everyone should just have a free-for-all of sin and degradation, all day long, every day. Their lifestyle should just be one big orgy of decadence and excess and hedonism and the satisfying of the lust of the flesh and the seeking of pleasure with absolutely no boundaries.

I'm really making an effort to avoid sarcasm here...well, at least I was before that last paragraph...but, honestly, that's what a lot of people must think I believe and preach. When some hear that you don't believe in the existence of a literal, burning hell in the center of the earth, they somehow assume you have no moral compass, whatsoever.

And if they don't totally think that, just try admitting publicly to them that, even though you have loved and served God your entire life, all that time you've had same-sex attraction.

That'll do it.

You may preach a message of reconciliation that is simply and sincerely celebrating Jesus' finished work on the cross... the declaring of the evangel or the GOOD NEWS...but what they hear you saying is something like, "Be sure to do some crystal meth with a prostitute before you knock over that 7-Eleven store tonight!"

Oops. There goes the sarcasm again.

My bad.

But I do get asked this question a lot: "Can you just do anything (bad) that you want and still be saved?"

Of course if you force me into a simple yes or no answer to that question, I would have to say yes; Paul said, *"All things are lawful for me, but not all things are good for me."*

Where sin abounds, grace much more abounds.

But, seriously, you may ask...what about pedophiles?

And satan worshippers?

And pornographers?

And serial killers?

And Democrats? (Sorry...more sarcasm in honor of all those who have sent me YouTube videos declaring that President Obama is the antichrist.)

But the Big Question is always the classic "Universalist" challenge:

"Do you think that Hitler is in heaven?"

Of course, that question ultimately comes from the paradigm created by having eaten from the "Tree of the Knowledge of Good and Evil" as opposed to the mindset that comes from the more optimal "Tree of Life"; in other words, as Paul said, *"to be carnally-minded is death, but to be spiritually-minded is life and peace."*

People who are spiritually-minded hear the message of reconciliation and think about how wonderful Jesus is.

People who are carnally-minded hear the same message and want to know what's going to happen to Hitler.

I especially hate the Hitler question because it takes the emphasis off the finished work of Christ and puts it on the horrible actions of a deranged maniac. And, certainly, the idea of seeing Hitler (or others of his ilk) happily walking down streets of gold in heaven with Moses and Elijah or David is completely unthinkable to anyone with a sense of sanity or morality.

But so is the thought of someone's sweet little grandma being sent to an eternity in hell with Hitler because she didn't pray the right prayer before she died, which is what some of these type people believe. I've even heard a televangelist preach that Mother Teresa and Gandhi are in hell because they weren't 'saved' according to what he believed was necessary for salvation.

Wow.

Really?

Mother Teresa?

"It's A Puzzlement"

Look, I don't have all the answers as to how things (like what to do with Hitler) get worked out in eternity; I just try to behold the Lamb of God Who takes away the sin of the world.

That being said, it's always interesting to me to observe how even people who believe in the triumph of the cross generally believe that the "really, really, really" bad people should be at least held more accountable, if not somewhat punished for their deeds. It's a normal response to try to get your head around some of the horrible acts that are committed every day by people in this world. Regardless of the fact that James said that if you are guilty in one point, you are guilty in them all, the sins of some people just naturally seem worse to us than the sins of others.

In eastern religions there is the concept of *karma* (basically what goes around comes around) to help people deal with the ramifications of evil. And reincarnation, which is based on the idea that if you do really bad stuff, you'll come back in another life as something really disgusting.

But western Christians have the concept of hell to help them psychologically deal with the need for justice to be served in cases of unspeakable wickedness.

Most of our western concepts of hell (especially the notion that there are degrees of punishment there) come from the *Divine Comedy,* better known as *Dante's Inferno* written by Dante Alighieri between 1308 and his death in 1321. Seen as one of the greatest works of world literature, the poem's imaginative vision of the Christian afterlife is a culmination of the medieval world-view as it had developed in the Western Church over the centuries and is much more responsible for shaping our ideas of eternal punishment than is the Bible.

I have read the transcripts from the murder trial of a diabolical man who intentionally ran over three little kids in a McDonald's parking lot around the corner from my house on a Saturday morning a few years ago. In the document were the recorded words of the mother whose three year old daughter was killed in the incident. She spoke directly to the man who had brutally snuffed out the life of her baby girl just days before her third birthday (laughing while he did it, by the way) and said to him that the Bible says that there is a "hottest place in hell" reserved for him and that she was going to laugh while she watched God throw him into it.

Now, I know that the Bible doesn't say anything like that, and you know what I believe about ultimate reconciliation, but, as a parent or just as a person who can't make sense of that kind of evil, I completely understood why she said that, and in some secret place in my heart or brain I hoped that she was right!

In other words, what I know by the spirit doesn't always jibe with what I feel emotionally, and if that were my little girl who was killed, I probably would have said the same thing, or worse!

In all honesty, I also really don't think I could ever forgive the man, nor would I even attempt to; only the "hottest place in hell" idea would give me some sense of psychological relief in the matter.

"You Can't Handle The Truth!"

But let's look at some literal interpretations of the Scriptures which define the conventional Christian ideas concerning who should really go to hell, which are generally taken out of context (and I'm using the King James Version to make my point because it sounds more profound and scarier).

First of all, the dividing of the sheep from the goats mentioned in Matthew 25 is about compassion, philanthropy and sensitivity to the needs of others...not about 'sin' as we think of it.

> *Then shall He say also unto them on the left hand, "Depart from Me, ye cursed, into everlasting fire, prepared for the devil and his angels: For I was an hungered, and ye gave Me no meat: I was thirsty, and ye gave Me no drink: I was a stranger, and ye took Me not in: naked, and ye clothed Me not: sick, and in prison, and ye visited Me not."*
> (Matthew 25:41-43)

The 'goats' in the parable are sent into the 'fire,' not because they were mass murderers or serial killers or sexual deviants, but because they didn't feed the hungry or clothe the naked or visit the prisoners. Yet we all know Christians who have never once entered a jail or prison to visit the incarcerated and have never once helped a homeless person in any way. But if you asked them if Hitler is in hell (or if the man I mentioned earlier is going there) they would more than likely say a definite yes, oblivious to the fact that Jesus said they were also going to hell!

Then in Luke 17, the rich man went to "hell" because he was rich, not because he committed any heinous acts (other than refusing to feed a homeless man). And Lazarus went to "heaven" (or Abraham's bosom), not because he prayed the "Sinner's Prayer" or confessed Romans 10:9, 10, but because he was poor:

> But Abraham said, "Son, remember that thou in thy lifetime receivedst thy good things, and likewise Lazarus evil things: but now he is comforted, and thou art tormented."
>
> (Luke 16:25)

Have you ever heard a preacher preach that all the indifferent rich were going to hell and all the suffering poor were going to heaven?

I haven't.

But that's what Jesus said, is it not?

So let me get this straight: Hitler is in hell because he committed genocide, Jeffrey Dahmer is in hell because he was a murderous cannibal, John Lennon is in hell because he wrote *"Imagine"* and the man who ran over those children is going to the "hottest place" there because of what he did...and yet Jesus said that calling someone an idiot or a fool is grounds for eternal punishment (according to conventional interpretation of Scripture).

> *But I say unto you, that whosoever is angry with his brother without a cause shall be in danger of the judgment: and whosoever shall say to his brother, Raca, shall be in danger of the council: but whosoever shall say, Thou fool, shall be in danger of hell fire.*
>
> (Matthew 5:22)

And do you know anyone who is afraid of anything? Well, apparently they're going to hell, too, right along with the serial killers and perverts:

> *But the fearful...and all liars, shall have their part in the lake which burneth with fire and brimstone: which is the second death.*
>
> (Revelation 21:8)

Thank God, Jesus was speaking metaphorically in each of these parables. With the sheep and goats analogy He was talking about people who are indifferent to the suffering of others who will have to go through a fiery trial sent to burn out their pride and force them to become empathetic and compassionate with those less fortunate. As I said, first century audiences would have understood what He was talking about.

And they knew where Gehenna was, so the idea of reaping what you sow was not confused in their minds with the fear of eternal damnation.

If you read John's Revelation in context, you see that The Lake of Fire is actually the purging of a merciful God...everything in His vision is symbolic: a crystal sea, a 7-headed dragon, a sun-clothed woman, a lake of fire, etc.

Compare John's revelation of it with that of Paul:

> *For no other foundation can anyone lay than that which is [already] laid, which is Jesus Christ (the Messiah, the Anointed One). But if anyone builds upon the Foundation, whether it be with gold, silver, precious stones, wood, hay, straw, the work of each [one] will become [plainly, openly] known (shown for what it is); for the day [of Christ] will disclose and declare it, because it will be revealed with fire, and the fire will test and critically appraise the character and worth of the work each person has done. If the work which any person has built on this Foundation [any product of his efforts whatever] survives [this test], he will get his reward. But if any person's work is burned up [under the test], he will suffer the loss [of it all, losing his reward], though he himself will be saved, but only as [one who has passed] through fire.*

(1 Corinthians 3:11-15 – AMP)

It's hard to understand with the natural mind declarations like *"I will have mercy on whom I will have mercy"* or *"The first shall be last, and the last shall be first."*

God's ways really are higher than ours.

But think about this: what if you had never heard of Adam or the Fall of Man and someone told you that the behavior of just one man brought death and condemnation upon all of humanity.

You might ask, "What in the world did he do to bring about such a horrible condition?

Did he kill millions of people?

Was he a pedophile?

Did he own slaves and lynch innocent people?

Was he a serial rapist?

An abortionist?

Did he torture people and ruin people's lives?"

And the answer would be, "No, he just ate a piece of fruit."

So, how do we deal with all of this? If you live in a very black and white world where you are absolute in your ideas of right and wrong, good and evil, it's easy. Just don't read the Bible a lot because it will disorient you in your polarization of what is right vs. wrong. I'll deal with some of that in the next chapter.

For me, the answer is in *working out my own salvation with fear and trembling, owing no man anything but to love him,* and basically just letting God be God.

My morality may not be yours (I was taught as a child that all cigarette smokers go to hell when they die), and yours may not be mine.

If you take on living your own life and spend your time trying to please God by becoming the best you that you can be, you won't really have time to deal with what's going on with the goodness or badness of other people.

Or even have an opinion about it.

CHAPTER SEVEN

"Who Wrote The Book Of Love?"

*If someone isn't what others want them to be,
the others become angry. Everyone seems to have
a clear idea of how other people should lead their lives,
but none about his or her own.*

— Paulo Coelho

Fat People Should Commit Suicide.

That's what I originally planned to name this book, but then thought better of it.

I know that title would have been a little too provocative and difficult to explain—it certainly would make the book unmarketable—but the idea comes from my frustration with so many fundamentalist Bible-thumpers who keep telling me, and people like me, that we need to "get back to the Bible" and "obey the commandments of God" and not "water down the Scriptures" with our message of grace and our liberal theology.

I'm fine with the concept of obeying the Bible in theory, but if we're going to take part of it literally and obey it to the letter, then we have to take all of it literally and obey all of it. You can't pick and choose. I'll get more into this in the chapter about Leviticus, but suffice it to say that there are a lot of people who use certain Bible verses to clobber other people of whom they disapprove, but they only pick and choose the verses that prop up their own agendas and protect and preserve their prejudices. Then they ignore the ones that don't matter to them.

I heard a man on Christian TV recently preaching against those who support gay marriage, and in his rant he said, "We need to get back to the BIBLICAL definition of marriage and not vary from it in any way!"

It's certainly within anyone's rights to be either for or against same-sex marriage. I've heard all the arguments, both pro and con, and I understand where everyone is coming from on the subject. It's a tricky one, at best.

But don't use the Bible to make your point for marriage between one man and one woman as we know it today if you want to have credibility.

I mean, whose marriage in the Bible can you set up as the example?

Adam and Eve weren't married.

Noah apparently had a wife, but we know nothing about her.

Abraham's wife, Sarah, was his sister, and she offered her servant, Hagar, to him so that he could sleep with her to impregnate her (which he did, because that kind of thing was customary then) and she gave birth to Ishmael.

Even a marriage like Isaac's and Rebekah's was an arranged thing (people marrying for love is a relatively new idea).

Jacob fathered the men who became the heads of the 12 tribes of Israel through 4 women (2 wives and 2 concubines).

Basically, all the married men of the Old Testament were polygamists with harems (Solomon had 700 wives and 300 concubines!). Within that context, I don't even know how you would define adultery for a man who already has multiple women available to him sexually.

So, you don't need to look in the Old Testament for marriage role models, because you won't find any.

And the New Testament is predominately about Jesus and Paul, neither of whom were married.

Jesus did, however, challenge the accepted concepts of marriage when He talked about the life and function of eunuchs (Matthew 19:10, 11). He said that some people couldn't understand or accept this, but there are those, like eunuchs, who aren't at all made for marriage as we know it. Many of my contemporaries believe and teach that He was referring to gay people in that discourse, but that's not settled in my mind at this point for reasons I will discuss later (see Chapter Ten).

The disciples had wives, but they were all nameless as far as the Bible is concerned.

We see a couple named Priscilla and Aquila in Paul's narrative who were apparently married, but we have virtually no information on them.

Even in the fifth chapter of Ephesians when Paul talks about husbands and wives, he ends that part by saying that he wasn't talking about marriage between a man and a woman, he was actually talking about Christ and the Church.

So if you want to argue against same-sex marriage, fine. Just say that you stand for 'traditional' or 'conventional' marriage... don't say you stand for 'Biblical' marriage because that may not be what you want at all.

Another preacher was defending the nuclear family and saying we need to model our families on what Jesus said.

Really?

What did Jesus say about the family?

He who does not hate father and mother cannot be my disciple. (Matthew 10:37)

Who is My mother and who are My brothers...those who do the will of God. (Matthew 11:48-50)

Do not think that I came to bring peace...I came to bring a sword... to set daughter-in-law against mother-in-law. (Matthew 10:34, 35)

He even told one man not to bother with taking care of his dying father when He said, *"Let the dead bury the dead."* (Matthew 8:21; Luke 9:60)

Many of those who say they believe and practice the whole Bible should probably go back and actually read it, especially before they start yelling at the ones who they think aren't doing it right.

Men In Glass Houses

I get a lot of correspondence in a week (email, letters, texts, phone messages), both positive and negative, but one day I got a private Facebook message from a man who was blasting me because, according to him, I didn't really preach obedience to the Bible because I had 'chosen' the gay lifestyle. He went on to say that if I don't obey all of the Bible I can't really call myself a Christian and that I was dangerous because I encouraged people to ignore the commandments of God.

His letter contained the usual vehemence and mean-spirited jargon that I get a lot from people in the conservative religious community, and I was just about to do my typical pushing of the delete button (I don't even read them anymore because they all just say the same thing) when I happened to notice his profile picture.

He looked like he probably weighed in excess of 400 pounds (maybe more)...he definitely appeared to be morbidly obese... and as I stared for a minute at the sour expression on his wide face perched atop all of his chins like a big, pink pumpkin,

I decided to make an exception and write him back a message that said something like this:

> Thanks for your message, sir, and you know what? You're absolutely right! We do need to get back to the Bible and start living it as we should. You've helped me see the light! I'm going to start telling all the gay people that they should repent for "choosing" their sinful "lifestyle"...and I'm also going to tell all the fat people...those who have chosen the fat lifestyle...that they should commit suicide because the Bible says *"...put a knife to your throat if you are given to gluttony"* (Proverb 23:2, NIV). We just can't, as you say, compromise the Scriptures. They must be obeyed! I just hope your suicide won't be too painful.

But then I decided not to send the message—just deleted it, because I'm a gentleman...maybe even a Christian—and just let him enjoy his smug self-righteousness and self-satisfaction in believing that he had put me in my place (and please don't write me to inform me that obesity isn't always the result of overeating, because that's not the point).

Then I blocked him on Facebook.

Look, I do love the Scriptures...with all my heart, in fact.

But I hate when they're taken out of context and used on other people as a weapon.

The best parts of the Bible are the ones that carry the GOOD NEWS.

That's what matters most and there's a lot of GOOD NEWS in there if you know where to look for it!

"Lift Every Voice And Sing"

With clever editing you can make the Bible say just about anything you want it to say.

It has no one particular voice because the Bible is NOT a book!

It is a *collection* of books...and ideas...and concepts...many of which are in contradiction to some of the others.

The protestant canon is a collection of 66 books written by 40 authors over a period of 1,500 years in different languages to different people groups in different generations for different purposes.

Therefore, the Scriptures must be rightly divided instead of wrongly connected.

In other words, each book must be judged in its own context and on its own terms, whether it confirms any other book or not. In this way, Biblical contradictions are not only acknowledged and accepted, they are expected.

I celebrate the tension caused by the conflicting viewpoints of the writers who had different paradigms of God; their contradictions make the Bible literally pulsate with life! And amazingly, in spite of the given contention, the confirmation of Jesus, the Christ, is still the glue that holds the whole collection together!

In this way, the Bible is actually a miracle.

But you can't ask what "The Bible" says about anything, because "The Bible" is a collection of books.

That would be like asking what the library says about something.

The library says a lot of things.

The library says 'War and Peace'.

The library says 'Of Mice and Men'.

The library says 'Alice in Wonderland'.

There is no official voice of the library.

That's why we have basically four different resurrection stories in the Gospels. The one constant among all the variables (number of women in the garden, number of angels, catastrophic events, such as an earthquake, or lack thereof) is that Jesus was in the grave and then He came out of the grave alive.

But there is no official resurrection story of record.

Contradictions abound between the leather covers.

For example, if you asked what "The Bible" says about using the title of Father, there is no definitive answer.

Jesus said to call no one "Father."

> *And do not call anyone on earth 'father, for you have one Father, and He is in heaven.*
>
> (Matthew 23:9 – NIV)

But Paul said just the opposite:

> *Even if you had ten thousand guardians in Christ, you do not have many fathers, for in Christ Jesus I became your father through the gospel.*
>
> (1 Corinthians 4:15 – NIV)

Peter tells wives that they are responsible for the salvation of their husbands...puts the onus entirely on the women by saying that their godly lives lived in front of their unbelieving spouses is more effective than The Word:

In like manner, you married women, be submissive to your own husbands [subordinate yourselves as being secondary to and dependent on them, and adapt yourselves to them], so that even if any do not obey the Word [of God], they may be won over not by discussion but by the [godly] lives of their wives, when they observe the pure and modest way in which you conduct yourselves, together with your reverence [for your husband; you are to feel for him all that reverence includes: to respect, defer to, revere him— to honor, esteem, appreciate, prize, and, in the human sense, to adore him, that is, to admire, praise, be devoted to, deeply love, and enjoy your husband].
(1 Peter 3:1, 2 – AMP)

But Paul says just the opposite:

But if the unbelieving partner [actually] leaves, let him do so; in such [cases the remaining] brother or sister is not morally bound. But God has called us to peace. For, wife, how can you be sure of converting and saving your husband? Husband, how can you be sure of converting and saving your wife?
(1 Corinthians 7:15, 16 – AMP)

No doubt, these next two passages are talking about two different things, but at first glance it appears that Jesus is telling us not to judge anyone/anything, while Paul is saying to judge everyone/everything!

But he who is spiritual judges all things, yet he himself is rightly judged by no one.
(1 Corinthians 2:15 – NKJV)

But the spiritual man tries all things [he examines, investigates, inquires into, questions, and discerns all things], yet is himself to be put on trial and judged by no one [he can read the meaning of everything, but no one can properly discern or appraise or get an insight into him].

(1 Corinthians 2:15 – AMP)

But Jesus says:

Don't set yourself up as a judge who takes the liberty of casually condemning others, or even as a critic who thinks that he or she has the right to criticize them, because when you do that, you set a universal law into motion that will inevitably bring negative things back into your own life. In other words, don't judge so that you may not be judged and criticized and condemned yourselves. For in direct proportion to your judgment, criticism and condemnation of others, you will be personally judged and criticized and condemned. It's just the way the law works. And in accordance with the measure you use to deal out to others...whatever you may deal out...it will be dealt out again to you. You define the terms of your own life in this sense.

(Matthew 7:1, 2 – GITN)

Jesus said to think and be like a child to be able to enter the Kingdom:

At that time the disciples came to Jesus and asked, "Who, then, is the greatest in the kingdom of heaven?" He called a little child, whom he placed among them. And he said: "Truly I tell you, unless you change and become like little children, you will never enter the kingdom of heaven. Therefore, whoever takes a humble place—becoming like this child—is the greatest in the kingdom of heaven.

(Matthew 18:1-4 – TNIV)

But Paul says:

> *Brothers and sisters, stop thinking like children. In regard to evil be infants, but in your thinking be adults.*
>
> (1 Corinthians 14:20 – TNIV)

Anyway, you get the point. The Scriptures are inspired...no doubt about it.

But they were spoken by the Holy Spirit through human beings—fallible, imperfect human beings—which is why, again, they must be rightly divided and why the contradictions in the Bible (the ones mentioned here are just a few) are found throughout the entire collection of inspired writings.

It's the same with the Gifts of the Spirit: the Gift of Prophecy is God speaking, indirectly, through human beings, which is why Paul told the Corinthians that prophecy must be judged by at least three elders for validation. Just because the message originated in the mind of God doesn't mean that what you hear spoken or see written down is the fullness of God's intention in saying it.

I love sefood, especially shellfish (even though it's an abomination to eat it...but more about that later). But I don't want to eat the shells of a crab, oyster, or lobster. Rightly dividing, to me, is like removing the shell from the crab legs to get to the delicious meat, or like peeling a banana or an orange to get to the sweet, edible fruit inside. When we rightly divide the Scriptures, we remove the shell of cultural bias and human opinion to get to the eternal food within that sustains and nourishes us spiritually.

That's why I don't waste my time arguing the Scriptures with narrow-minded religious people who have never made the effort to break open the shell/husk/peel/outer layer of dogma to find the real Word within the Scriptures...the GOOD NEWS that is at the center. They have never *tasted and seen that the Lord is good,* so they don't even know what I'm talking about when I share revelation.

Straight Talk

As I've already said, this isn't just a book about what it really means to be gay...it's a book about understanding in general, which is why I need to address some of these issues so that I can be done with the subject and move on to other things in future books. Thanks, straight people, for bearing with me through these parts.

I will say, however, that I have received scores and scores of letters from heterosexuals who tell me that they watched my coming out video and were greatly moved by it...many times to tears...and that it inspired them to be authentic in their own lives. Here's an example:

> *Just saw the CNN report tonight with Pastor Swilley. I don't normally email, blog, etc., however, I must share that I found his interview VERY refreshing. Never have I seen a pastor, especially of a megachurch, be so honest. I am a wife and a mother and a heterosexual. I do not attend church, mainly because of too many churchgoers wanting to cast the first stone and be so judgmental of others. I would absolutely go to church if this man was at the pulpit. He is obviously very intelligent, and I am so pleased to see him have the courage to step forth and handle his "coming out" so professionally and with confidence. Pastor Swilley, you will hear many harsh words in the coming days, weeks and months. You know what you did was right, and hopefully this will give the strength to others to stop trying to live their lives according to how others think they should. Perhaps you will even spare a suicide. Stay strong!!!*

Anyway, in the following chapters I'm going to go through every reference the Bible makes to homosexuality, but it's not for argument's sake.

I have found when I show someone what these passages say in the original Greek, or explain the original context of some of the phrases used—when I show them that a reference made to boy prostitutes used in pagan temple worship got translated as 'homosexual' or 'effeminate' in some translations—that religious people will hear the truth as I have explained it and respond by saying, "Well, I see your point, but I STILL say it's wrong and God hates gay people!"

It's why Jesus said not to cast your pearls before swine... why He said to shake the dust off your feet and move on to a more receptive audience when you're rejected. Some people are never going to see beyond their own bigotry, and they are convinced that God shares their prejudices.

But I don't argue about the Bible and sexual orientation for the same reason I don't argue the pros and cons of the virtues of slavery.
The Bible supports slavery...even in the New Testament.

Paul said, *"Slaves (not servants), obey your Masters"*; in the very same chapter where he says *"Christ is all and is in all"* (Colossians 3:11), he says to obey your Owner *"in everything,"* meaning even if they mistreat you. He wrote to the Corinthians and Galatians about it; he also said that, even if a believing slave's master is also a believer, the slave should not assume the master isn't superior to him.

That's what The Bible says about slavery, yet in modern times, no Bible-believer (no matter how conservative) would invite me into a debate about the validity of slavery. Even though the Bible supports it, our culture has moved beyond that...the verdict is in...nothing else to discuss about it.

So we rightly divide the Scriptures about slavery by removing the antiquated, archaic shell of a certain Scriptural viewpoint on human rights that no longer relates to us as a society.

The Bible says you can sell women as property.

Moses said that if your daughter is raped, you can sell her to the rapist (Deuteronomy 22:28,29). No one today, no matter how "Christian," would engage me in an argument about whether women were personal property or human beings. The Bible says it, but our culture has moved beyond that mindset. We have rightly divided the Scriptures on that subject.

So...I love the Scriptures, but slavery is still wrong!

I believe the Bible, but I would never sell my daughter to anyone, much less a man who raped her!

And I know what the Bible says, but God still loves gay people... just as they are.
OK, let's knock out this next part...

...maybe set some people free...

...share some GOOD NEWS!

CHAPTER EIGHT

"We Gotta Get Out Of This Place"

Now this was the sin of your sister Sodom: She and her daughters were arrogant, overfed and unconcerned; they did not help the poor and needy.

(Ezekiel 16:49 – TNIV)

Sodom and Gomorrah.

No one wants to live there.

I certainly don't.

The realities of those strange cities from the distant past and their bizarre inhabitants certainly have little, if anything, to do with me and my life as a civilized man who lives in the twenty-first century. The only way they could have any less relevance to me or anyone like me is if they had been built on Mars.

And yet I've been asked about them endlessly...for some reason, there are people who somehow connect the full truth of my life (or that of others like me) with the events of the story in Genesis of God's wrath being poured out on Sodom and Gomorrah.

It's funny how the minds of some people work.

But, in fact, these cities are so much a part of our collective consciousness, at least subliminally, that it's virtually impossible for any one of us to ignore them...so we will discuss these often-misquoted and generally misunderstood Biblical references.

Sodom.

The mere mention of the name of this ancient and doomed metropolis evokes a feeling of darkness and basic ickiness, even though it was actually one of many geographical areas that was destroyed by God in the days of the Old Testament.

Because of the way language has evolved with the coining of terms like 'sodomy' and 'sodomite,' there is just something about Sodom that sounds dirtier and more evil than Tyre and Sidon or Jericho or any of the other wicked cities mentioned in the Bible, like Ninevah, or even Babylon.

Gomorrah, it seems, was basically just guilty by association because we know nothing specific about it.

But they were the original sin-cities and they were obliterated as a result of their wickedness...if you take the stories of the Old Testament literally.

We can see from the above Scripture verse, however, that Ezekiel clearly had a different take on what, exactly, was the sin of Sodom. His perspective certainly was different from that of the conventional wisdom. This prophet said that the sins of the city were arrogance, gluttony and indifference to the poor and needy.

And yet the city of Sodom has become inextricably linked over the centuries to people having same-sex attraction and to the perceived hatred and intolerance that God apparently has for such types. This is in spite of the fact that homosexuality is never once mentioned in the Scriptures as the reason for God destroying it.

In the Hebrew Bible, Sodom was a city destroyed by God because of the evilness of its inhabitants. The clearest texts on the sin or sins for which Sodom was destroyed are found in

Ezekiel and in the book of Jude (I'll get to that in a minute). But here's the big question:

QUESTION #6: *Did God destroy Sodom and Gomorrah because of homosexuality?*

ANSWER #6: *No, He destroyed it because Abraham stopped at 10!*

The story of the city of Sodom's destruction (again, nothing is really ever said about Gomorrah), and of Abraham's failed attempt to intercede with God to prevent that destruction, appears in Genesis, chapters 18 and 19.

No specific sin is given as the reason for God's intense wrath, but in the story, Abraham asks God if He will spare the city for the sake of 50 righteous people who might be found there and God says, without hesitation, an absolute yes.

Then Abraham asks God if He will spare it for 40 and, again, God says yes.

Then he asks if God will spare it for 30...again, God says yes.

Then there is a request for the city's salvation for the sake of 20 righteous people and God immediately agrees to the proposition with no argument, whatsoever.

Then Abraham, seeing that God is so agreeable to giving the city a reprieve, asks if He will spare it for the sake of only 10, and God, again, agrees.

But then, for some reason, Abraham stops at 10.

Even though God was apparently totally open to showing mercy to the city, Abraham never thinks to continue in that vein and say, *"Will You just spare it for my family...or even just for me?"*

The pattern in the Old Testament was that God would typically pronounce judgment on a city/nation/group of people (usually through a Prophet) and then wait for the city to repent or for an intercessor to rise up and call for mercy to thwart the judgment.

He told Moses in a similar story concerning the Israelites, *"Now leave me alone that my wrath may wax hot against them!"* implying that if Moses would ask for mercy, He would have no choice but to give it.

And He did.

In Ezekiel, He said that He would spare a nation for the righteousness of just one man... *"I looked for A MAN to stand in the gap and make up the hedge, but could find none, and so I sent destruction..."*

But for some inexplicable reason, Abraham just stopped the bidding at 10. Even though God was clearly flexible and open to an alternative, Abraham never asked for anything beyond the sparing of the city for ten righteous people and, in so doing, sealed the fate of Sodom and Gomorrah.

It's not like this was the original "God Hates Fags" campaign in which God was out to rid the earth of all the homosexuals regardless of anything Abraham or anyone else had to say about it. The subject of homosexuality never comes up in the discourse between God and Abraham.

The connection between Sodom and homosexuality is derived from the depicted attempt of a barbaric mob of city inhabitants to gang-rape the male guests who come to visit Lot.

Much has been said and written of the sinfulness of that instance. For the original writers of the Biblical account (it has been speculated), the actual sin may have consisted mainly in the violation of the obligations of hospitality, which in ancient cultures was a very big deal. But this view does not take into consideration that before the 'guests' arrived in the city—before any 'hospitality' could have been rendered—its destruction was already planned (Genesis 18:17). So we probably need to rule that out as being the only reason for God's wrath, even though in The Book of Judges (19-21), we find a similar account where a city is almost totally destroyed in punishment for a mob of its inhabitants raping a female.

Many times in the *Pentateuch* (Torah) and in the Major and Minor Prophets, writers use God's destruction of Sodom to demonstrate His awesome power.

This happens in Deuteronomy 29 (no mention of homosexuality)...

...in Isaiah 1, 3 and 13 (no mention of homosexuality)...

...in Jeremiah 49 and 50, Lamentations 4 (no mention in either)...

...Amos 4:11 (no mention)...

...Zephaniah 2:9 (no mention)...

Deuteronomy 32, Jeremiah 23:14 and Lamentations 4 reference the sinfulness of Sodom but do not specify any particular sin.

Specific sins which Sodom is linked to include adultery and lying (Jeremiah 23:14)...

...impenitence (Matthew 11:23)...

...careless living (Luke 17:28)...

...fornication (Jude 1:7, KJV)...

...and an overall 'filthy' lifestyle (2 Peter 2:7), which word *(aselgeiais)* elsewhere is rendered in the KJV as "lasciviousness"

(Mark 7:22; 2 Corinthians 12:21; Ephesians 4:19; 1 Peter 4:3; Jude 1:4) or "wantonness" (Romans 13:13; 2 Peter 2:18).

In Ezekiel 16, a lengthy comparison is made between Sodom and the Kingdom of Israel: *"Yet you have not merely walked in their ways or done according to their abominations; but, as if that were too little, you acted more corruptly in all your conduct than they."* (Ezekiel 16.47 – NASB)

There is no explicit mention of any sexual sin in Ezekiel's summation, and "abomination," as we will see in the next chapter, is used to describe many sins.

Don't Miss The Point

But here's the bottom line: whether the story of Sodom and Gomorrah has any relevance whatsoever to modern day people with same-sex orientation or not, the fact is that if you went to visit the "gayest" city in America tonight...

San Francisco...

West Hollywood...

South Beach...

Atlanta...

wherever...you wouldn't have to worry about the locals gathering outside your door, threatening to gang-rape you in the streets!

Gang-rape, whether done publicly or privately, is both immoral and illegal, as it should be. In fact, rape of any kind is generally condemned by both the gay and straight communities, and this kind of threat made by these primitive people wasn't even about sex anyway; it certainly wasn't about love. For these barbarians, it was about intimidation... about letting the outsiders/intruders know that they weren't welcome.

And even though this occurrence wasn't the reason for the city's destruction (because it had been sentenced to annihilation prior to this event), it definitely shows you how grossly dark they all were.

And if it doesn't prove how irrelevant the lives of these crazed savages are to those of responsible gay people living in the modern world (who are or should be against rape), the thing that removes it even farther from anything we can identify with is that they weren't even trying to rape *people!*

According to Jude 1:7, they were after "strange flesh," which is rendered in better translations as "celestial beings."

> *Even as Sodom and Gomorrah, and the cities about them in like manner, giving themselves over to fornication, and going after strange flesh, are set forth for an example, suffering the vengeance of eternal fire.*

In 40 years of counseling, I've heard just about everything— every kind of sexual issue you can imagine—but I never met anyone who wanted to rape an angel!

Then the story gets even more weird because Lot, when he hears the threats of the would-be rapists, offers to send his virgin daughters out to the men so that they could sexually assault them instead of the celestial guests in his house!

Then, later in the story, these same daughters get their father drunk and attempt to seduce him so that he could impregnate them!

Suffice it to say, no one in their right mind, gay or straight, wants to live in a place as messed up as Sodom and Gomorrah! So please don't bring up Sodom and Gomorrah to me to make your point about what you think about God and His relationship to gay people. As a man with that orientation, I can't relate at all to wanting to gang-rape angels or mortals or anyone at all, for that matter...and even though I know a lot of gay people, I've never met anyone who was cool with that idea on any level. In that sense, these cities are just as removed from gay people, both intellectually and emotionally, as they are from straight people.

And as a father, I certainly can't relate to the idea of seeing my daughters as 'things' or as property...commodities that can be sent out, against their will, to be raped by strangers!

The fact that God was willing at all to spare the place, when He entertained Abraham's incomplete intercession for it, is really quite remarkable.

So if you want to exercise your homophobia and clobber a gay person with some Scriptures, just by-pass this story in Genesis altogether.

That gay person is more than likely just as grossed out by the story as you are and can't relate to it any more than you can.

Next question...

CHAPTER NINE

"Why Don't We All Just Get Stoned?"

As long as we continue to live as if we are what we do, what we have and what other people think about us, we will remain filled with judgments, opinions, evaluations, and condemnation. We will remain addicted to putting people and things in their "right" place.

— Henri J.M. Nouwen

ABOMINATION!!!

If I had a nickel for every time that word has been included in a letter, e-mail, text, phone message or blog comment addressed to me from a "Christian" (especially in the months right after I came out), I would probably have enough money for a nice little vacation somewhere.

Hey...wait a minute...I thought this book was about GOOD NEWS, you say; what's all this ABOMINATION stuff about?

It is! It is about GOOD NEWS...and I'll get back to that topic... just got to sort through all the religious/legalistic stuff so that I can get back to the good part.

I have to address the system that uses the Scriptures as a weapon on the vulnerable...and that may get a little tedious in the next several chapters...but I promise it all ends with GOOD NEWS, so stay with me through these parts if you can...

Now, where was I?

Oh yeah...ABOMINATION!!!

That word gets thrown around a lot, especially when the religious intolerant want to make a point to prop up their personal prejudices.

It shouldn't be surprising, though...the Bible does, in fact, use the word quite a bit.

Here are but a few of the many Bible references to it:

Cheating is an abomination (Micah 6:10).

A proud look is an abomination (Proverb 6:16-17).

A lying tongue is an abomination (Proverb 6:17; 12:22).

Hands that shed innocent blood are an abomination (Proverb 6:17).

A wicked scheming heart is an abomination (Proverb 6:18).

Feet that are quick to sin are an abomination (Proverb 6:18).

A false witness that speaks lies is an abomination (Proverb 6:19).

A sower of discord among brethren is an abomination (Proverb 6:19).

A false balance or scale is an abomination (Proverb 11:1).

The sacrifices of the wicked are an abomination (Proverb 15:8; 21:27).

The proud of heart are an abomination (Proverb 16:5).

Condemning the just is an abomination (Proverb 17:15).

Divers, dishonest weights are an abomination (Proverb 20:10, 23).

Divers, dishonest measures are an abomination (Proverb 20:10).

Refusing to hear the law is an abomination (Proverb 28:9).

The prayers of a rebel are an abomination (Proverb 28:9).

Eating the flesh of a peace offering on the third day is an abomination (Lev. 7:18).

Taking ornaments from idols when they are being destroyed is an abomination (Deuteronomy 7:25-26).

Any idolatrous practices are abominations (Deuteronomy 12:31; 13:14; 17:4; 18:9; 20:18; 29:17).

Offering an imperfect animal to God as a sacrifice is an abomination (Deuteronomy 17:1).

Re-marriage of former companions is an abomination (Deuteronomy 24:1-4).

Cheating others is an abomination (Deuteronomy 25:13-16).

Making images or idols is an abomination (Deuteronomy 27:15).

Incense offered by hypocrites is an abomination (Isaiah 1:13).

Eating unclean things (pork, shellfish, etc.) is an abomination (Isaiah 66:17).

Offering human sacrifices is an abomination (Jeremiah 32:35).

Robbery is an abomination (Ezekiel 18: 6-13).

Oppression of others, particularly the poor or vulnerable is an abomination (Ezekiel 18: 6-13).

Violence is an abomination (Ezekiel 18: 6-13).

Breaking vows is an abomination (Ezekiel 18: 6-13).

Lending with interest to a brother is an abomination (Ezekiel 18: 6-13)

Sleeping with a menstruous woman is an abomination (Ezekiel 18: 6-13).

Hardness of heart is an abomination (Ezekiel 18: 6-13).

Injustice is an abomination (Ezekiel 18:6-13).

Things highly esteemed by man are an abomination (Luke 16:15).

There are even more abominations mentioned, but you get the idea...

Of course, the "abomination" that many fundamentalist Christians feel most obligated to either inform me of or remind me of is mentioned in two verses from Leviticus: Leviticus 18:22 and Leviticus 20:13, which basically say that if a man has sex with another man, they should both be killed (nothing is mentioned about Lesbians anywhere in the Old Testament).

And the ones who want to use the 'A-word' to beat up the gays are not just limited to the fundamentalists. People with virtually no knowledge of the Scriptures...people who otherwise never even think about the Bible...suddenly become authorities on Holy Writ when it comes to the subject of homosexuality. They don't care about much of anything the Bible has to say about much of anything else, but, boy, when you start talking about the gays, they start quoting the Bible like the house is on fire and water is ten miles away.

A Trip To The Library

As I've already said, "The Bible" doesn't talk about homosexuality...at least not as some kind of theme that runs through the entire collection of books. There are a handful of verses in which Moses, Paul and Jude used words that got translated into our modern understanding of people with same-sex attraction (and in this chapter I want to highlight the two verses where Moses used the 'A-word'), but "The Bible", as a collection of books, not only doesn't condemn homosexuality, it doesn't even mention it.

OK, now for some of the tedious part I warned you about... my apology for that, but I need to make a point here, which is this: the way some homophobic preachers talk, you'd think "The Bible" just talks non-stop about people with same-sex attraction, and that's just not the case.

So let's look at it, book by book.

Moses is the primary author of Genesis through Deuteronomy (known in Hebrew as The Torah). He compiled the pre-flood manuscripts of the early chapters of Genesis, along with other manuscripts from which Genesis is comprised. He wrote the other four books of the Torah during the 40 years Israel wandered in the wilderness.

In Genesis, there is the story of Sodom and Gomorrah that we've already discussed.

The book of Exodus never mentions homosexuality.
The book of Leviticus mentions it twice, as I've said (referring to homosexual men only).

The book of Numbers never mentions homosexuality.

The book of Deuteronomy never mentions homosexuality.

Joshua wrote most of the book bearing his name, while Samuel completed the final portion of that book, in addition to Judges and Ruth. Samuel edited his own additions, plus portions of the Torah. Joshua never mentioned homo-sexuality, so the book of Joshua never mentions homosexuality.

The book of Judges never mentions homosexuality.

The book of Ruth never mentions homosexuality.

Samuel, who also wrote much of the initial chapters of 1 Samuel, never mentioned homosexuality, so that book never mentions it...unless you consider the story of David and Jonathan (more about that later)...

The prophet Isaiah wrote the remainder of 1 Samuel, as well as 2 Samuel, 1 and 2 Kings, and Isaiah. Much of the work by Samuel and Isaiah was done by collecting and compiling older accounts recorded by prophets close to when the events took place. For example, Elijah had written much of what Isaiah compiled as part of the books of the Kings; 1 and 2 Chronicles, Ezra and Esther were recorded by Ezra who was primarily used by God to edit, compile and canonize the entire Old Testament. So, 1 Samuel never mentions homosexuality...

2 Samuel never mentions homosexuality.

1 Kings never mentions homosexuality.

2 Kings never mentions homosexuality.

1 Chronicles never mentions homosexuality.

2 Chronicles never mentions homosexuality.

In the book bearing his name, Ezra never mentions homosexuality,

...neither does Nehemiah...

...nor does the book of Esther.

The book of Job was most likely written by Job, and he never mentions homosexuality.

King David wrote more than half of the Psalms and he never mentioned homosexuality (at least not in a negative way.)

Others portions of that book were written by Moses, Hezekiah, Solomon and others, and none of the Psalms mention homosexuality.

King Solomon also wrote Proverbs, Ecclesiastes and the Song of Solomon, and he never mentioned homosexuality in any of those books.

Isaiah, in his book, never mentioned homosexuality.

Jeremiah wrote the book bearing his name and authored the book of Lamentations, and he never mentioned homo-sexuality in either of them.

Ezekiel, in his book, never mentioned homosexuality.

Daniel, in his book, never mentioned homosexuality.

Hosea, in his book, never mentioned homosexuality.

Joel, in his book, never mentioned homosexuality.

Amos, in his book, never mentioned homosexuality...

neither did Obadiah...

...nor Jonah...

...nor Micah...

...nor Nahum...

...nor Habakkuk...

...nor Zephaniah...

...nor Haggai, Zechariah or Malachi.

That does it for the Old Testament, and I will devote an entire chapter to everything that Jesus said about homosexuality in the next chapter, so I won't go into Matthew, Mark, Luke, or John here. After that, we'll also discuss what Paul said about it, and we've already discussed what Jude said about it in the previous chapter, so that does it for the New Testament, as well.

Playing The Leviticus Card

But for the average, run-of-the-mill homophobe, the two verses in Leviticus are enough to make the case for the hatred and intolerance of gay people. After all, Moses said to kill them, right?

Well, yeah, he did...but he said a lot of things that were just as extreme...mentioned a lot of types of people who should be executed under his system (including a lazy son who won't work for a living!). God may have indeed given him the Ten Commandments on Mt. Sinai, but by the time we get to the end of The Torah, Moses has presented us with 613 commandments!

Wow, that's a lot of trips up to the top of the mountain!

So if you believe that the two verses about same-sex relationships should be observed and obeyed, what about these other things that Moses said in Leviticus? If you're going to play the Leviticus card, you have to play the whole hand with commandments like this:

Don't let cattle graze with other kinds of cattle (Leviticus 19:19).

Don't have a variety of crops on the same field (Leviticus 19:19).

Don't wear clothes made of more than one fabric (Leviticus 19:19).

Don't cut your hair nor shave (Leviticus 19:27).

Any person who curses his mother or father, must be killed (Leviticus 20:9).

If a man cheats on his wife, or vice versa, both the man and the woman must die (Leviticus 20:10).

If a man sleeps with his father's wife, both he and his father's wife are to be put to death (Leviticus 20:11).

If a man sleeps with his wife and her mother, they are all to be burnt to death (Leviticus 20:14).

If a man or woman has sex with an animal, both human and animal must be killed (Leviticus 20:15-16).

If a man has sex with a woman on her period, they are both to be *"cut off from their people"* (Leviticus 20:18).

Psychics, wizards, clairvoyants, and so on are to be stoned to death (Leviticus 20:27).

If a priest's daughter is a whore, she is to be burnt at the stake (Leviticus 21:9).

People who have flat noses, or are blind or lame, cannot go to an altar of God (Leviticus 21:17-18).

Anyone who curses or blasphemes God should be stoned to death by the community (Leviticus 24:14-16).

And my personal favorite: anyone who fails to tithe on their produce/income must get caught up on it and be charged a 20 percent penalty (Leviticus 27:30, 31); wow, if people still practiced that, I wouldn't have any financial challenges with my church!

Makes you wonder why there are so many people wanting to site Leviticus for gay bashing, but they never mention these other rules.

How strange.

It's common that a fundamentalist "Christian" will generally blow off these old precepts with something like, "Jesus came to change (fulfill) the Law(s), so these are obsolete and outmoded and we don't need them"; I find that they are adamant about that law thing when it comes to the subject of the tithe penalty(!)... but throughout Leviticus, God states that these laws are to be followed forever.

Most people with some Bible knowledge are at least vaguely familiar with The Ten Commandments listed in Exodus (although I find very few people, even among fundamentalists, who can actually quote them). But there are also often-overlooked rules in Deuteronomy which nobody ever seems to mention (at least not to me), such as:

Anyone who dreams or prophesies anything that is against God, or anyone who tries to turn you from God, is to be put to death (Deuteronomy 13:5).

If anyone, even your own family, suggests worshipping another God, kill them (Deuteronomy 13:6-10).

If you find out a city worships a different god, destroy the city and kill all of it's inhabitants...even the animals (Deuteronomy 13:12-15).

Kill anyone with a different religion (Deuteronomy 17:2-7).

And another of my personal favorites that I already mentioned (Deuteronomy 21:18-21): if you have a son who is stubborn and won't obey his parents—even if your only issue with him is that he eats all the groceries in the house and drinks some—you are to take him to the elders of the city and tell them that he's a lazy glutton and have them stone him with stones until he is dead!

Wow...that's some serious disciplinary action for grown kids who still live at home with their parents.

OK, OK...enough...I could add more, but you get the point... reading the Laws of Moses gets oppressive pretty fast, so let's move on.

Makes you hungry to hear some GOOD NEWS.

You may ask: if so many things in the Bible are so clearly irrelevant to life in our modern world, why believe any of it at all?

Because there's hidden treasure in these books, and if you know how to rightly divide them, you can find a whole lot of GOOD NEWS within their pages!

Really!

Paul wrote to the Romans and said that the purpose of the Law was that it was to implode...to self-destruct as it were, so that it could ultimately show us how wonderful Christ is...

For what the law was powerless to do because it was weakened by the sinful nature, God did by sending his own Son in the likeness of sinful humanity to be a sin offering. And so he condemned sin in human flesh...

(Romans 8:3 – TNIV)

See? I told you this was still about GOOD NEWS!

But just remember...don't play the Leviticus card, because you might end up getting stoned, just like the rest of us.

Regardless of what Moses said or what the Law said or what Moses said through the Law, God is real and God is love.

Amazing isn't it?

Nearly sounds like the Bible is sending us mixed messages, but at the end of the day it really isn't.

It's still all about the GOOD NEWS!

CHAPTER TEN

"The Sound Of Silence"

Therefore whoever hears these sayings of Mine, and does them, I will liken him to a wise man who built his house on the rock.

(Matthew 7:24 – NKJV)

Words are important.

According to the Genesis story, the worlds were *spoken* into existence...literally created by words (Hebrews 11:3)...

To a Christian, the words of Jesus should be the most important words ever uttered...words to live by...words on which to build one's spiritual house.

In most Bibles, His words are printed in red to give them the honor and prominence they deserve.

The words of Jesus Christ are the most important ones in the Bible.

In the last two chapters, we've discussed a story in Genesis which many people believe has relevance to people with same-sex attraction, and two things that Moses said that many modern-day Bible believers like to quote to show their disapproval of gay people. We'll get to Paul's Epistles next, but right now we come to what I believe is perhaps the most important chapter in this book.

When Jesus said in His teaching *"You strain at gnats and swallow camels,"* He was talking about knowing the difference between what may or may not be important to God, and what is absolutely vital to Him. To me, that means that, as a Christian, if Jesus talked about it, then it's vital to me...if He never mentioned it, I have to assume it's low priority, if not completely immaterial, to Him. Thank God for what David and Isaiah and Abraham and Peter and the rest of the Bible authors said, but at the end of the day, what matters most...maybe all that really matters...is what Jesus Christ said.

Jesus talked about a lot of things—a nearly endless array of a variety of topics—His Father...His purpose for coming to the earth...the Kingdom of God...religion...the Pharisees...His parables...love...forgiveness...baptism...prayer...faith...sowing and reaping...the Temple...Abraham...sin...the destruction of Jerusalem...servitude...the rich...the poor...unbelief...taxes... the Sabbath...fishing...the lilies of the field...living water...the Scribes...the heart of man...prophecy...Samaria...loving your enemies...sparrows...harvest...the Holy Spirit...Jonah...feeding the hungry...money...death...healing the sick...worry...fasting... casting out demons...the anointing...Gehenna...foxes...the cost of discipleship...satan...sheep and goats...judgment... John the Baptist...turning the other cheek...the Two Great Commandments...the Law...Noah...stewardship...the end of the age...His death, burial and resurrection...and on and on...

He was eloquent when He wanted to be...confrontational when He needed to be.

His words were so revolutionary that they said of Him, *"Never a man spake like this man."*

He said, *"The flesh profits nothing, but the words I speak are spirit and they are life..."*

...and *"Now are you clean through the words I have spoken to you."*

That being said, I want to talk about Jesus' words...about what

Jesus taught concerning people with same-sex attraction. As I said, we've looked at what Moses said about it, and we'll look at what Paul said about it, but the Kingdom of God is built on the words of Christ...Jesus' words...the words in red...the words which are definitive. They are the most significant of all.

He said that heaven and earth would pass away, but His words would remain, so I think it's of the utmost importance that we, as Christians, examine and take to heart every single thing that Jesus said on this and every other subject.

The life of Jesus, the Christ, is of course revealed to us through four biographies that we call "The Gospels"...The Gospels according to Matthew, Mark, Luke and John...

First, let's look at everything Jesus said about homosexuality recorded in the 28 chapters of the Gospel of Matthew*:

That's everything.

Now let's look at His complete teaching on the subject...all that Jesus said about homosexuality...in the 16 chapters that comprise the Gospel according to Mark:

That's every bit of what Jesus said about it in Mark.

Let's also examine the entire teaching of Jesus on God's attitude toward homosexuality in the 24 chapters that make up Luke's Gospel:

That completes His entire teaching on the subject in the three Synoptic Gospels.

And, finally, let us read every single thing that He said about homosexuality throughout the 21 chapters in the Gospel of John:

That completes Jesus' entire teaching on the subject.

The Gospels are so important, especially if you really want to be a disciple...a follower of Jesus Christ. That's why we need to take the time to observe and meditate on all the teachings of our Lord.

Jesus said that out of the abundance of the heart the mouth speaks, so we need to pay attention not only to the things that Jesus did in His earth-walk, but especially to the things that Jesus said, because they indicate what was abundantly in His heart...what was really important to Him.

We also need to pay attention to the things He didn't say.

Selah.

*As I said earlier, I personally do not believe that Jesus' teaching on eunuchs in Matthew was in reference to homosexual people, mainly because He said that some people are eunuchs by choice, and I absolutely do not believe that sexual orientation is a choice. However, many of my contemporaries—some of them much more academically astute than I—do believe that He was talking about gay people there. In fact, I know several learned scholars who believe and teach that every time the Scriptures mention eunuchs throughout both Testaments that they're really talking about gay people. I have no argument with them, just a difference of opinion. But, for the sake of point, I will include the much-debated passage from *Matthew In The Now,* chapter 19... hopefully it will bring some clarity to the subject for you...

[3.] *And while He was in the area, the Pharisees came to Him again and put Him to the test by asking, "Is it legal and right for a man to dismiss his wife...to divorce her for any reason that he may have?"*

4. *He replied to them, "Have you never read in your Scriptures that He Who made them from the beginning made them male and female?*

5. *This is why a man has to leave his father and mother at some point and be united and bonded to his wife...and when that happens, the two of them become, in a sense, one single entity,*

6. *so that they are no longer two separate physical bodies, but actually become one new one. And if a particular union between a man and a woman is, indeed, God-ordained, then no human being should do anything to create a disconnect between what God has put together."*

7. *They shot back at Him, "Well if marriage is so special...if, indeed, it is a God-created thing, then why did Moses make it so practical and easy to get a divorce? According to his law, all a man has to do to get out of a marriage is to send his wife a written notice and then just simply dismiss her from his life and be done with her, altogether."*

8. *He said to them, "Moses set up this system basically because of the hardness of your hearts...specifically, your insensitivity to women. He permitted you to simply dismiss your wives with no regard for required responsibility to them because you have had no concept of covenant. But in this Moses did not have the heart and mind of God, considering that this self-serving male convenience was not in God's original plan.*

9. *But I say to you that whoever just casually dismisses his wife for no legitimate reason and marries the next available woman who comes along, really is only committing adultery with her. His shallow flippancy in such a case shows that he has no understanding of the seriousness of covenant. The situation is somewhat different if the wife has been unfaithful to her husband, but the real issue is still about the apparent disregard of covenant. So if a man marries a woman just because she was dismissed*

for her unfaithfulness to her husband, he is still just committing adultery with her if there is no genuine commitment to the covenant of marriage."

[10.] *The disciples, listening in on this conversation, said to Him, "If that's really what marriage is about...if covenant is really that important...if God takes it that seriously...then no man in his right mind would ever want to get married! What would be the point of limiting your options by binding yourself to that kind of commitment?"*

[11.] *But He said to them, "Marriage is for men...not for boys. That's why not all men can accept this concept. It's for those who are mature enough to understand and appreciate the value of human, adult relationships.*

[12.] *But it also requires a certain kind of maturity to understand that this kind of relationship isn't for everyone. There are some asexual men who, from birth, never seem to give women or marriage a thought. Other men may have been intentionally emasculated for cultural purposes, or for other reasons. And still others are single and celibate for spiritual pursuits...as if they were married only to the Kingdom of/from the heavens. Whatever the case, it requires insightful maturity to comprehend that not everyone takes the same path or has the same needs in these matters. If you can receive this, you will be able to live and let live."*

Amen.

CHAPTER ELEVEN

"Listen To What The Man Said"

For we know in part, and we prophesy in part...
– The Apostle Paul

I love Paul.

My preaching finds its source nearly entirely in the New Testament, divided pretty much right down the middle...about half of it from The Gospels and the other half from Paul's Epistles.

I guess if I had to claim a favorite chapter in the Bible it would probably be Romans, Chapter 8, part of his letter to the church at Rome *(There is therefore now no condemnation...the whole creation groans...waiting for the manifestation of the sons of God...).*

I love His post-resurrection revelation of Christ; I consider it to be pristine.

I love his independence...the fact that, after his conversion, he went to Arabia for three years to develop his own theology/ideology instead of going to Jerusalem to be mentored and/or influenced in any way by the original Apostles. He thought for himself, nearly to the point of being unteachable, and this is in spite of the fact that he learned at the feet of Gamaliel, a teacher who was to Israel and to Judaism what Socrates and Plato were to the Greco-Roman world.

I love that he never stopped defending his Apostleship, even though it was questioned, challenged and debated for as long as he lived because he wasn't one of the original twelve.

I love his mystical side...the part of his gift that produced the kind of imaginative writing we find in the first chapter of Ephesians...that sort of out-of-the-box thinking that enabled him to present concepts such as "The Body of Christ" or the notion that Jesus was crucified *"before the foundation of the world."*

I personally believe that he wrote the book of Hebrews and, if indeed he did, I think it's amazing how he took the symbolism and typology of the Old Covenant in that book and made it relevant to those who were not originally of the seed of Abraham.

I love his faith and tenacity...that bulldog kind of can-do perseverance that enabled him to survive beatings, being left for dead on more than one occasion, shipwrecks, and all kinds of intense opposition.

I love his universalist teaching...when he said things like *"Christ is all and is in all,"* or when he said that Christ was even in the Scythians (the most primitive of the barbarians), a concept that would have been considered outrageous to most civilized people at the time.

I love that he never talked about hell or eternal damnation and confirmed the promise of ultimate reconciliation by saying that eventually *every knee will bow and every tongue will confess.*

I love that he continued to evolve as his tradition gradually (and sometimes reluctantly) bowed to his revelation—something to which I can definitely relate.

I love his flawed humanity...the fact that he struggled with his own beliefs and was sometimes inconsistent, like when he circumcised Timothy, even though he constantly insisted that circumcision didn't mean anything under the New Covenant.

I love his candor and transparency...the inner conflict that he openly shared with his readers in Romans 7 (*"O, wretched man that I am..."*), the fact that he had issues with his ego and was often intolerant and inflexible with others, like when he had a permanent falling out with Barnabas over Mark. He could be totally full of himself at times, and yet he could write the ultimate masterpiece on love in 1 Corinthians 13.

I love that he set an example of knowing *"how to be abased and...how to abound,"* how to be content in every state in which he found himself and, in that context, could say that he could do all things through Christ who strengthened him.

I love that he said that those who are in the ministry should be financially supported by the ministry, but also did what he had to do, making tents to supplement his income when it was necessary.

I love that he eventually made peace with his life (*"by the grace of God I am what I am..."*) and even made peace with his death (*"to live is Christ, and to die is gain"*).

I could write a whole book about Paul, and one day I might.

But not everyone holds my high opinion of him, even among theologians and scholars...some of the greatest thinkers in history...mainly because Paul's writings seem to be in conflict with some, if not much, of what Jesus taught.

This is not a problem for me personally because, as I've already said, I embrace and even celebrate Biblical contradictions...the exchange of ideas that comes from different paradigms (THE BIBLE IS NOT A BOOK! THE BIBLE IS A LIBRARY OF BOOKS!).

To make my point, here are a few quotes. I neither fully agree nor fully disagree with any of them, even though I do (and always will) love Paul and his mind and his teaching.

"...Paul is in effect the first Christian heretic, and his teachings, which become the foundation of later Christianity, are a flagrant deviation from the 'Original' or 'pure' form extolled by the leadership. Whether James, the 'Lord's brother,' was literally Jesus' blood kin or not (and everything suggests he was), it is clear that he knew Jesus...personally. So did most of the other members of the community or 'early Church,' in Jerusalem including, of course, Peter. When they spoke, they did so with firsthand authority. Paul had never had such personal acquaintance with the figure he'd begun to regard as his 'Savior.' He had only his quasi-mystical experience in the desert and the sound of a disembodied voice. For him to arrogate authority to himself on this basis is, to say the least, presumptuous. It also leads him to distort Jesus' teachings beyond recognition, to formulate, in fact, his own highly individual and idiosyncratic theology, and then to legitimize it by spuriously ascribing it to Jesus."

"As things transpired, however, the mainstream of the new movement gradually coalesced, during the next three centuries, around Paul and his teachings. Thus, to the undoubted posthumous horror of James and his associates, an entirely new religion was indeed born, a religion that came to have less and less to do with its supposed founder."

From the book, *The Dead Sea Scrolls Deception*
by Michael Bajgent and Richard Leigh
(Corgi Books, London, 1991)

*"Paul was the great Coryphaeus,
and first corrupter of the doctrines of Jesus."*
– Thomas Jefferson

"Where possible he (Paul) avoids quoting the teaching of Jesus, in fact even mentioning it. If we had to rely on Paul, we should not know that Jesus taught in parables, had delivered the sermon on the mount, and had taught His disciples the 'Our Father.' Even where they are specially relevant, Paul passes over the words of the Lord."

– Albert Schweitzer

*"Paul hardly ever allows
the real Jesus of Nazareth to get a word in."*

– M Carl Jung

As I previously mentioned, Jesus said to call no man "Father" on the earth; Paul, however, insisted that He was to be considered and called a father by his followers, even though they may have had thousands of instructors.

Jesus elevated the status of women and seemed to enjoy their company...all kinds of women...prostitutes...a woman caught in adultery...a woman with an issue of blood...a woman who had had five husbands and was living with a man to whom she wasn't married.

The first person Jesus called to the ministry of proclaiming His resurrection was a woman, Mary Magdalene.

Paul told women to keep silent in the church...didn't allow them to usurp authority over men...told wives to submit to their husbands.

Women apparently found Jesus to be approachable...a safe place for them in a very patriarchal world in which they were considered to be not much more than objects...

Suffice it to say, a harlot never felt comfortable enough to wash Paul's feet with her hair!

And when it comes to the subject of homosexuality, as I said in the last chapter, it didn't even seem to be on Jesus' radar screen...but it was definitely on Paul's.

Not By Bread Alone

I am willing to accept and believe without reservation that *"all Scripture is given by inspiration"* (which is something that Paul said to Timothy in a letter), but there's no way to know whether or not Paul ever intended for his personal letters, many of which were largely administrative in nature, to be considered Holy Writ.

Would he have been surprised to know that down through the centuries his Epistles to certain, specific churches would become what they eventually became to the world? Would he be further surprised to find out that his letters to a few individuals—individuals whom he personally mentored—would attract such a larger audience...that they would be included in what became The Bible?

May I go so far as to ask if he would be surprised to discover that some people would actually come to a point where they began to consider the Bible to be "THE" only Word of God?

I know that many Christians consider these questions to be a dangerous, slippery slope because they have been taught to accept the canon of Scriptures as an absolute of perfection; most likely these same people have been taught to not question anything at all when it comes to the Bible...that questions are really just blasphemy in disguise.

But I really and sincerely wonder if Paul considered his own letters to be the Word of God.

There's no way to know that, of course; there's even some dispute among some theologians and historians as to whether or not he actually penned all of the letters that we assume he actually wrote.

I say all that, not to discredit the writings of Paul (as I said, I love them), but to put them in some perspective. I think that legitimate truth can withstand some honest questioning and real examination.

For what it's worth, here's how I see it: in my opinion, the Scriptures are definitely inspired but not necessarily infallible. Some Christians have a meltdown when I say that, but I honestly think that many people have made the Bible into an idol—a sort of religious icon that must be worshipped as a fourth addition to the Holy Trinity—and have elevated it to a point to which it should never have been elevated.

Look, the Bible no doubt *contains* and *archives* a lot of the Word of God—a lot of what He said in the past to different people and people groups for whatever was happening *at that time*—but **the** Word of God is a proceeding (present tense) Word...a now Word...as it is written, *"Man shall not live by bread alone, but by every word that PROCEEDS from the mouth of God"* (Matthew 4:4 - NKJV).

But I do believe the post-resurrection revelation of Christ that Paul wrote about is real, supernatural, other-worldly. I don't believe it came from the mind of a brilliant man; I believe that it came from heaven.

That does not mean, however, that I think Paul was the "go-to" guy for advice on human relationships, especially human sexual relationships.

Was he anointed? No doubt.

Called? Absolutely.

An Apostle? Yes, because Christ continued to appoint people to ministries and *"gave gifts unto men"* even after He was no longer revealed in the flesh as Jesus, the Son of Man...just as He continues to do today.

Was Paul who he said he was? Yes, I believe so.

Did Paul have 'issues'? You bet! Just like you and I do; in fact, he talked about them a good bit.

In a word, when I want to know more about the revelation of Christ, Paul is my guy.

When I need clarity on the realities and complexities of human sexuality, not so much.

Why? Well, here's a little of Paul's perspective on romance, marriage, sex, etc. You be the judge.

He referred to natural, physical desires as the thing that was waging a certain *war in his members.*

Read Romans 7, in the Amplified Bible and tell me it doesn't sound like he was referring to some kind of personal, sexual conflict when he talked about the problem with his flesh.

Paul just didn't seem to like women at all, for some reason. Well, if he indeed liked them, he at least was insistent on keeping them in their place, as he saw it...and this is in spite of the fact that Jesus clearly and continually went against the social mores of His day and liberated women; it was an integral part of His message.

Paul said that the ONLY reason to get married was if you were so weak in character that you just couldn't live without sex (*"it is better to marry than to burn"*), as if there is nothing to love, companionship, romance, or relationship in a marriage... nothing to two people building a life together because of compatibility and mutual interests. And, yes, I know about Ephesians 5 *("Husbands, love your wives, even as Christ also loved the church")*; I've been using that passage in wedding ceremonies for decades, and I already discussed that. Paul said that he wasn't talking about marriage there.

I dare say that if the only reason you are married today is because you just simply can't contain your burning lusts and need a sexual facilitator to help you deal with them, then you probably don't have a real marriage anyway. To me, that kind of arrangement sounds more like prolonged prostitution than real matrimony.

I'm just sayin'...

But that was Paul's idea of the reason to get married. He wore his own celibacy as a badge of honor and looked down on those who didn't have the same 'gift' that he had.

He even defined the act of marital sex by using the decidedly dismal and unromantic phrase, *"render...due benevolence."* Don't agree with me about that? Fine. You straight, married guys, next time you want to be intimate with your wife, try saying something to her like, "Honey, get in here and render me some 'due benevolence' so that I can stop burning in lust!" and see how the night goes for you. I dare say that line is not going to work for the average married woman!

But Paul didn't empathize with women.

In fact, the entire Bible, whether inspired or not, was written *by* men *to* men, because women were kept illiterate then, as a rule. All of it is written from a male perspective; even the parts that are inspired by the Holy Spirit are filtered through the paradigm of a man.

And when it comes to dealing with the issues of people with same-sex attraction, I would add that the Bible was written *to* straight men *by* straight men...men who had no comprehension, whatsoever, of what it really means to be gay.

"You're A Mean One, Mr. Grinch"

In the Preface to this book, I mentioned about how many times two passages from Paul's letters—one to the church at Rome and one to the church at Corinth—have been sent to me (as if I've never read them) in letters and messages from "Christians" who wanted to straighten me out (no pun intended).

In the days and weeks following my coming out and the media coverage of it, there was an absolute avalanche of mail that came in from all over the world, especially after the video of my message to the church went viral on the internet, and most of them were from furious "Christians."

The reason I put the word "Christians" in quotations here is that nearly every one of these letters that contained references to Romans 1 and 1 Corinthians 6 (with the exception of maybe less than I could count on one hand) also contained the vilest, most vitriolic and vulgar language I've nearly ever heard in my life. No mention of prayer...no mention of love...and for those who think of people with same-sex attraction as fallen reprobates, no mention of any kind of offer of restoration, whatsoever.

Just hostile hate-speech, sent and received over and over and over again.

Typically, the hundreds and hundreds of letters from people who sent me references to the abominations mentioned in Leviticus (see Chapter Nine) were relatively tame but, for some reason, the people who have quoted Paul to me are some of the angriest, meanest homophobes I've ever heard from.

I mean, seriously, if you could read some of the stuff I've gotten from "Christians" you'd know that it's not over the top or too politically correct to have people lobby for hate-crime legislation for gay people...there are some very scary heterosexuals out there!

I've deleted or thrown away all of their letters now because they're just so dark but, really, you just wouldn't believe some of the things that the Paul-quoters have said to me: liberal usage of the word 'fag' and 'faggot,' explicit references and descriptions of what they imagine intimacy between two men is like (no mention of lesbianism; they generally seem to be fine with that), and lots and lots of references to demon possession, hell, judgment, sodomy, false prophets, signs of the times, and many, many threats of AIDS as a judgment from God.

I'm reluctant to empower this thought, but my favorite was the one that read:

> HOW CAN YOU DARE TO CALL YOURSELF A PASTER [sic]?????????? YOU NEED TO READ THE BIBLE AND RECEIVE JESUS CHRIST AS YOUR PERSONAL SAVIOR AND LORD!!!!!!!!!!! SOMEBODY NEEDS TO CAST THE DEVIL OUT OF YOU SO YOU CAN GET SAVED!!!!!! YOU ARE GOING TO HELL!!!!!!! GET RIGHT WITH GOD AND READ LEVITICUS AND ROMANS 1 YOU GODDAM FAGGOT!!!!!!!!!! REPINT [sic]!!!!!!!!!!
> FROM, A "REAL CHRISTIAN"

Truth be told, I hate to include that in a book that's supposed to be about GOOD NEWS, but I think it just really says it all.
On the other hand, it's that kind of talk that actually makes me want to stay in the ministry and double my efforts to share some GOOD NEWS with the world because, if that's what a "real Christian" sounds like, Jesus still has a lot of work to do with His followers! As the song says, "Where is the love?"

Speaking of Jesus, He said that the thing that would separate the sheep from the goats and send the goats into the fire ("hell" for those of you who believe that's what He meant) was whether or not you visited the sick and incarcerated, clothed the naked, and fed the hungry.

I dare say that if I had gone on national TV and announced to the world that, regardless of the commandments of Jesus Christ, I wanted to make a declaration that I would never, ever feed another hungry person, or visit a prisoner in prison, or provide clothing for someone who was indigent for as long as I live, I probably would have gotten no reaction from it at all (wouldn't even be a blip on the radar screen of the "real Christians") because that kind of stuff is generally pretty low priority with them.

And to the Paul-quoters I would also interject that he said he preferred that all people spoke in tongues (1 Corinthians 14:5), but I don't expect to hear the Southern Baptists speaking in tongues any time soon...are you kidding me? The denominational Pentecostals hardly speak in tongues any more!

Guess it doesn't matter what Paul said about that, unless you're a Charismatic Baptist and I don't even know if there are still any of those around.

Paul said that women should cover their heads in church, but I don't see a lot of women wearing hats on Sundays...at least not like they used to.

Guess it doesn't matter what Paul said about that, unless you're a traditional Roman Catholic.

Paul said women should have long hair and men should have short hair.

Guess it doesn't matter what Paul said about that, unless you're from an old-school Holiness church.

Paul said a good bit about the required marital status and family-life of bishops, pastors and elders, but I don't think a lot of the people on Christian television know or care a lot about that; I don't know...maybe their ex-wives do.

I could go on and on about some of Paul's commandments that don't seem to push any buttons with most church people these days, but when you tell them that you have always had same sex attraction...well, OK...I think I've made my point.

When In Rome

Romans 1:18-32.

You can read it for yourself (if you don't have a Bible, just Google it).

As I said earlier, I assume that the people who have cut and pasted this passage to me so many times must think that in 40 years of preaching I never came across these verses.

Let me tell you...I've read them.

Many, many times.

And here's the deal: I could go verse by verse and show you that he was referring there to ancient pagan practices of temple worship—people who were worshipping graven images of *birds, animals and reptiles*—and, as I said in an earlier chapter that Sodom and Gomorrah has no more relevance to my life than it does to the life of a straight man, I could add that this reference has no relevance to my life as a gay, Christian man living in the twenty-first century, whatsoever.

I mean, I'm gay, but I promise you I've never worshipped the statue of a bird...

...or of a reptile...

...and I don't know any gay people who have, either.

In other words, pagan temple worship of idols didn't turn me gay. I do not identify with these people of antiquity in any way.

If I were to take this whole passage literally, I would have to deduce that people who aren't "thankful" turn gay...that people who "do not retain God in their knowledge" turn gay.

Sorry, that's not true.

I'm very thankful...always have been...still gay.

I retain God in my knowledge every day of my life...always have...still gay.

Nothing 'turns' you gay...you either are or you aren't.

I could also point out that these people who were *"given over to depraved minds"* (KJV uses the word 'reprobate') were not identified by who they were in relationship with; the litmus test of the reprobate mind was this:

> *Furthermore, just as they did not think it worthwhile to retain the knowledge of God, so God gave them over to a depraved mind, so that they do what ought not to be done. They have become filled with every kind of wickedness, evil, greed and depravity. They are full of envy, murder, strife, deceit and malice. They are gossips, slanderers, God-haters, insolent, arrogant and boastful; they invent ways of doing evil; they disobey their parents; they have no understanding, no fidelity, no love, no mercy. Although they know*

God's righteous decree that those who do such things deserve death, they not only continue to do these very things but also approve of those who practice them.
(Romans 1:28-32 – NIV)

Again, a literal interpretation would conclude that people who are full of envy are *"given over to a reprobate mind."*

Same goes for people who are in strife...

and greedy people...reprobate!

Gossipers...reprobate!

Slanderers...reprobate!

Arrogant people...reprobate!

People who boast...reprobate!

People with no understanding...people who show no love or mercy (in other words, most of the Christians who have sent me hate-mail)...

...even people who are disobedient to parents; I don't know, did you ever disobey your parents? Well, welcome to the world of the reprobate mind!

Wow...if I take these words literally, I would have to presume that most of the whole world, including people in the church, are gay!

I could even take you to the first verse of Chapter 2 and show you that Paul said if you even judge someone for doing or being these things, that you are the exact same thing!

You, therefore, have no excuse, you who pass judgment on someone else, for at whatever point you judge another, you are condemning yourself, because you who pass judgment do the same things.

(Romans 2:1 – NIV)

So I guess the appropriate response to the hundreds of "Christians" who have sent me a cut and paste of this passage because I'm gay would be, "I know you are, but what am I?"

Bottom line...I could show you all these verses in their proper, historical context, along with studies of original Greek words—and there are many books already written out there that do a better job of that than I could, authored by people who are more educated than I—but it has been my experience that if you present a more educated way of thinking to someone whose prejudices have been established and deeply ingrained by what they think the Bible says, they generally aren't swayed by your words at all.

The response from them is usually something like, "Well, I guess you're right about that passage, but I *still* say..."

And sometimes they get really, really, really mad about it.

And when they get violently angry about it, you understand why Jesus said not to cast your pearls before swine, because they will *"trample them underfoot, and turn and rend you."*

In 1 Timothy, Chapter 1, Paul indeed writes to his protégé and lists the kinds of rebels for whom the law is made, and included in that list, along with liars, murderers and fornicators, is what the KJV interprets as *"them that defile themselves with mankind";* some modern translations use the word 'homosexual' or 'sodomite'...

But the verse that has been quoted to me the most often is probably 1 Corinthians 6:9, in which Paul gives a partial list of those who will not "inherit the kingdom."

I guess some people think I've never read it.

In this list, the KJV uses the word 'effeminate' (which is the Greek word *malakoi* which actually means 'soft' or 'weak' or 'spineless'), and the term *"abusers of themselves with mankind,"* which refers to the type of physical mutilation that was practiced among pagans in bizarre sexual/worship practices among young male temple prostitutes. Some modern translations make a difference here between homosexual and sodomite used in the same sentence.

Whatever the case, many Paul-quoters don't seem to be all that concerned with the fornicators, idolaters, adulterers, thieves, people who covet, drunks, revilers and/or extortioners, but they want to make sure the gays know they're not going to heaven (which is not what that verse is talking about if you read in it context), as they interpret this verse to mean. By the way, "not inheriting the Kingdom" and "not going to heaven" are two different things...but I'll save that for later.

Paul made many of these types of lists in his letters, but the ones found in 1 Timothy and in 1 Corinthians are the ones that contained words often seen as being relevant to what it means to be gay by many traditionalists.

Again, here's the point...

I could examine these words and split hairs over meaning and context here, but the bottom line is: you're basically going to see what you see in the Scriptures, no matter what I say, or anyone else, for that matter.

As I said, many books have already been written that examine these things, and even more similar articles are available on the internet...and the books and articles on both sides of Biblical interpretation on these matters don't always agree.

Think what you need to think about Paul...or about legalism...or about what Paul said that Jesus didn't say...

When I use the phrase "You're a mean one, Mr. Grinch," I'm not calling the Apostle Paul the Dr. Seuss character by that name; I'm talking about the religious people who think they can speak for Paul when it serves their purposes of oppressing people and putting them in religious bondage.

As I said, I love Paul.

Still.

But, at the end of the day, trust your own heart on these matters...it's what Paul himself called *working out your own salvation with fear and trembling.*

Need to go meditate a minute on some GOOD NEWS now.

CHAPTER TWELVE

"You Better Think!"

*I regard Christian and Jewish fundamentalism,
and all other forms of fundamentalism, as the enemies
of God—and I hope you'll quote me on that.*
                                                        – Arthur Hertzberg

They finally got Osama Bin Laden.

It was nearly ten years after the fact...ten years after September 11, 2001...but they finally got him.

As an American, I joined in with the rest of the country in breathing a collective sigh of relief in knowing that the despot had been removed from the world stage, and I applauded the obviously successful efforts of our Commander-In-Chief and of the amazing soldiers who executed a virtually flawless raid on Bin Laden's Pakistani mansion/compound.

It's regrettable that it took so long to find him (especially since he had obviously been hiding in plain sight the whole time), but it's even more regrettable, as far as I'm concerned, that we are still at war in Iraq and Afghanistan at the time of this writing.

But, at least he's gone.

Being as patriotic as the next guy, I was moved by the spontaneous celebrations that broke out at the White House and in Times Square and at Ground Zero the night that the President announced that Bin Laden had been taken out, and I certainly don't want to be insensitive to the pain of the families who lost loved ones on that horrible September morning in '01—families that will never have full closure from the atrocities of that day, no matter who is assassinated—but I was quite sober when I heard the news.

Relieved? Yes.

Happy? Not really...at least not totally...

At the time, I expressed this same sentiment on my blog and, for the most part, my thoughts were very well received...but there were those who misunderstood my point completely (so what else is new?) and sent me numerous statistics of the many deaths for which Bin Laden was responsible...some even accused me of wanting to invite him to my house for dinner and become best friends with him.

(sigh)...

Certainly, no one needed to convince me what a bad guy he was—9/11 broke my heart—but I'm used to people missing the point on a lot of subjects that I discuss; being misunderstood comes with the territory when you have a large platform through which you express your ideas, especially ideas that aren't really mainstream.

Anyway, the point is this: we live in such an unkind world...people killing one another, hating one another...the longer I live, the more intolerable this reality becomes. So, even though what was done in Pakistan at Bin Laden's compound apparently had to be done, I couldn't and can't in good conscience really rejoice in the death of anyone, no matter how evil they are.

Am I glad he's gone?

No doubt about it.

I'm glad to know that we don't have to dread another of his videos coming out that shows he's still alive and still a threat to our safety.

But I am grieved that we live in a world where this kind of thing still has to happen at all.

What does this have to do with GOOD NEWS and the other things I've discussed in this book? Just that the world needs a revelation of the GOOD NEWS now more than ever!

Let me give that statement some context for this chapter...

The President gave a short but brilliant speech to the country the night of the assassination in which he pointed out that Osama Bin Laden did not and does not represent Islam, and he was right about that.

In fact, Bin Laden killed more Muslims than he did any other group.

But where my mind went immediately was that the real enemy was not Osama Bin Laden...or any other person, for that matter.

The real enemy was and is religious fundamentalism.

Fundamentalism kills...be it Muslim or Christian or that of any other religious persuasion.

The Crusades...

The Spanish Inquisition...

The Holocaust...

The violence between Protestants and Catholics in Ireland...
The Ku Klux Klan...

The Taliban, etc...

It's all about religious intolerance that stems from fundamentalist interpretations of Holy Writ.

I'm proud to be an American.

I'm proud of our President and of our troops.

I love my country and I want it to be safe.

But I'm really, really tired of religious fundamentalism and all the hatred and death that it inevitably causes.

Terrorism happens every day in the name of religion; believe me, I know of what I speak.

"In The Beginning"

Fundamentalist Christians read the Bible with no sense of context, no concept of how to discern the 'spirit' of the letter, and so they just continue to fixate on the parts of the written script with which they agree, even though what they focus on is nearly always *"the letter that kills."*

For example: Of course God created the universe.

Call it intelligent design, or whatever, the fact is that science cannot answer all of our questions about the origin(s) of everything. Even though there is clearly and undeniably some evolution that takes place in every species, including that of humans (if you don't believe it, ask yourself why people have wisdom teeth), there is just no way that everything on the earth, including all of the different species of animals, could have evolved into such a sophisticated and complex bio-system.

And this is no doubt a very simplistic way to approach it, but I think it's obvious that we didn't come from apes for the very simple reason that there are still apes. If simians, regardless of how 'human' they often seem in demeanor and mannerism, were just a link in the chain, then why didn't they eventually all evolve into homo sapiens?

So yes... *"In the beginning God created the heavens and the earth."*

That's a given.

But that doesn't mean that science is wrong in its assertion that the earth is older...much, much older...than 6,000 years, as many traditional creationists believe.

Did God speak the worlds into existence? I believe He did, but that doesn't mean that I rigidly hold to the idea that He created the earth absolutely and definitely in only six 24-hour periods and then rested on the seventh.

If Moses were here today, I believe he would explain to those mainstream Bible believers who read the Genesis account strictly through a fundamentalist paradigm that he was speaking poetically when he wrote the creation account in Genesis 1. The ancient Hebrews, of course, would have understood that. Moses wasn't there when God created everything, so he had to find a way to explain the creation of all things in a way that his readers could understand.

The important thing is that, ultimately, God created everything... whether or not he did it in six days or six seconds or six million years. The fact is that creation is an act of divinity and the product of the God-kind of faith.

When Christians argue over the "six days" creationist stand versus the idea that God created everything through a process of evolution, they miss the point, entirely.

Bottom line, it was a miracle, and God did it.

The Whole Truth And Nothing But The Truth

Were Adam and Eve the first people on the earth?

Clearly not...and that's according to the Scriptures.

Moses indeed begins his narrative about God's covenant with humanity with only Adam and Eve and their children, but in the fourth chapter of Genesis (after Cain kills Abel) we hear of other people who are already alive and living somewhere else in the earth.

After the murder, Cain is sentenced to become a vagabond, roaming around with no place to settle down. So he tells God he is afraid that, as he travels the earth, when other people find out that he committed fratricide, they will want to kill him, too.

So God puts a mark on him as a warning to anyone else who might want to do him harm because they had gotten wind of his terrible crime...and the mark means that everyone else who already lives on the earth is to leave Cain alone.

Other people already lived on the earth?

Who?

The Genesis account isn't clear about that but, whoever they were, they obviously had the ability to communicate, gossip, and threaten other people with murder.

And in the following verses we see that Cain ends up going to a place that already existed, east of Eden, called Nod.

There was apparently already a civilization there in Nod, and Cain finds a woman in that place whom he marries and they become the parents of Enoch.

If you rigidly hold to the idea that Adam and Eve and their children were the first people, then you can't make any sense of this part of the story...and you also have to conclude that Cain committed incest by marrying his own sister. In fact, if you follow this fundamentalist notion as an absolute, you would have to believe that all of the children of Adam and Eve married and had children with their siblings.

Typically, fundamentalists miss the point of this story, entirely.

The point is not the literalness of the historical facts of Adam's family; I believe the point is that God wants to be (and is very much) involved in the affairs of human beings...that our actions have consequences...and that even in punishing Cain for his wicked deed, God still shows him mercy and offers him protection.

These are important and powerful concepts...the multi-faceted moral of the story...the 'truth' of the Genesis account, if you will.

Was there a flood that destroyed the entire world except for the eight Hebrew people on Noah's Ark?

There most likely was a terrible and devastating flood in antiquity that caused mass destruction, and telling about it became part of the oral tradition of ancient peoples. But it seems impossible to believe that the flora and fauna, not to mention all the people of the earth, were all destroyed in one universal, global flood.

First of all, Moses, no doubt, would have believed that the earth was flat when he and whoever else wrote Genesis relayed the story of the Great Flood. Their idea of the whole world would have been just the world that they knew about.

Furthermore, if there were only eight Hebrews saved on the entire planet, then where did Asians and Africans and Europeans and all the indigenous people of the earth come from?

The point of the story, as far as I'm concerned, isn't whether or not there were actually and literally two kangaroos and two zebras and two grasshoppers, etc. on the ark...the point of the story (and again, fundamentalists seem to miss this, altogether) is that one man can make a difference...indeed, one man can save the world!

If there were not a Noah story, there could be no Gandhi story...

...or Dr. Martin Luther King, Jr. story...

...or Rosa Parks story...

...or the story of any other individual who has made an impact on humanity to the point that history was actually altered by their actions.

In reality, there couldn't even be a Jesus, the Savior, story without a Noah story.

Look, I'm not saying that the stories of the Bible are fables... I personally believe that there is an element of truth in all of them.

I can believe that there was a literal Adam and a literal Eve, but not to the point that I overlook and misunderstand the symbolism of their personalities in the story of God's relationship to humanity.

I believe that people who take the Bible so literally that they accept every single word of it as an absolute, completely bypass the importance and significance of the power of story-telling.

Jesus certainly understood and employed the art of story-telling, because He taught nearly entirely in parables, and the effectiveness of His colorful tales have little to nothing to do with whether or not there was an actual/literal Unjust Judge or Prodigal Son or Good Samaritan.

And if you read the four Gospel accounts of the Resurrection of Jesus, you basically find four different versions of the events of that day...there is no official story of record, and you'd think there would be considering that the Resurrection is perhaps the most important event recorded in the Bible.

But the one constant of the four stories is that Jesus was dead and then He was alive. That's what matters...not how many women were in the garden, or how many angels there were, or whether or not there was an earthquake, or whether or not Jesus commissioned Mary Magdalene to tell the disciples about it.

Fundamentalism fixates on the facts of the story and ignores the inspiration and relinquishes the revelation of the narrative.

So...is the Bible true or not?

The Bible certainly *contains* truth, and ultimately reveals *"The Truth,"* but it must be rightly divided before any truth can actually be found in it.

And, as I've already said...if you know where to look, you find that it's truthfully just loaded with pretty much nothing but GOOD NEWS!

Chapter Thirteen

"Momma Always Said, 'Stupid Is As Stupid Does'"

Genius may have its limitations,
but stupidity is not thus handicapped.
– Elbert Hubbard

God made Adam and Eve...not Adam and Steve!

If I've heard it said once, I've heard it a thousand times or more.

We discussed Adam and Eve a little in the last chapter (and nothing about sexual orientation issues, in case you didn't notice), but in this chapter I will need to discuss sexual orientation a lot.

Believe me, this isn't really what I want to be talking about, but I have to address some of the nonsense that has been thrown at me and answer some of the questions about being gay and Christian that I've gotten over and over again from straight people, especially in the last year. This being the twenty-first century and all, I shouldn't even have to deal with this stuff, but you gotta do what you gotta do...

So bear with me.

OK...first, let me say, once and for all, that **HETEROSEXUALITY IS ALIVE AND WELL!**

I make this simple and obvious statement for the sake of the many people who, for whatever reason, write, e-mail, call, text, or post on my blog to remind me that God created Adam and Eve, not Adam and Steve.

I'm not sure what this tired and overused phrase is supposed to mean, really, or what it is supposed to accomplish. I guess it is said to me and to people like me for the purpose of possibly snapping my mind back to the reality of the creation story of Genesis 1 and to hopefully change my sexual orientation...as if a statement like this could alter my thinking about the long-held truth of my life or my beliefs about human sexuality.

But I've heard the Adam and Steve thing said so much—not just to me, but also publicly from pulpits across America over the years and in television debates over gay rights issues—that I have to deal with it and make some observations that will hopefully bring a little clarity on the subject (and maybe stop people from saying it so often).

And since I mentioned the preachers, let me interject here that there is a dark, manipulative side to the preaching ministry that most laymen are unaware of. By that I mean that if a preacher needs to stir a crowd and get a certain reaction from his audience, there are certain phrases and buzzwords—a sort of verbal bag of tricks, if you will—that can really work a crowd if you know how to use them.

The theme of homophobia is most times a sure thing when you want to get a rise out of a congregation of mainstream Bible-believers these days, and the 'Adam and Eve, not Adam and Steve' thing is the catch-phrase that seems to be the most memorable and effective.

It's been my experience that, typically, when a ministry puts an excessive amount of emphasis on 'Family Values' instead of being Christ-centered in its message, you can just expect gay-bashing to be central in the preaching.

And when a fundamentalist preacher gets really wound up and starts yelling about the end of the world and the collapse of civilization as we know it, you can pretty much predict that somewhere in his sermon (rant), the gays are going to get blasted more than any other group. They'll get blamed for every earthquake and hurricane that's recently happened (with the usual references to the wrath of God), then you'll generally hear some historically-inaccurate information about the founding fathers, finished off with a menacing threat that the gays are out to get your children.

Indeed, if a fundamentalist man of the cloth wants to work his narrow-minded, misinformed crowd into a frenzy, 'Adam and Steve' are pretty much a sure thing for him and a nearly sure-fire way for him to gain supporters.

Then you'll usually hear him make a pitch for a big offering, with something said like "Give to this ministry so that we can keep the perverted homosexuals in their place and protect your children from them!"

And it usually works.

Fear sells.

When a preacher uses the Bible to make gay people seem evil and threatening to an assembly of ignorant homophobes who are convinced that they are the "real Christians," it's like throwing meat to hungry dogs.

The haters just eat that stuff up.

But please allow me to say some things about all this. I can't make you agree with me about it; I can only say what I truly believe and let you judge it for yourself.

But, if you can, try to hear me out without prejudice.

OK...let me reiterate that heterosexuality is not going anywhere.

Procreation is not in any danger.

The overwhelming majority of the world is straight and always will be, and men and women will always continue to date, fall in love, get married, have sex, have babies and do whatever else straight people do.

Despite what you regularly hear from the Christian right, the world is not turning gay.

There is no 'gay agenda' to fear in the sense that gay people are trying to recruit heterosexuals to turn to a 'gay lifestyle' (which also doesn't exist, by the way, but more about that later).

Nobody 'turns' gay.

It's just not possible.

And, yes, I've read the first Chapter of Romans (see Chapter Eleven) where Paul talks about men leaving women for men and women leaving men for women (the only hint at a reference to lesbians in the Bible, by the way), and all I can tell you is that whatever pagan temple sex rituals for worship that he was talking about there has absolutely no relevance to my life, whatsoever, nor to the life of any gay person alive today that I know.

I think I've already said this in a previous chapter, but for the sake of point I will repeat that homosexual experimentation between heterosexuals does not make those heterosexuals gay. For example, if two straight men in prison end up being sexual with each other in some way, they're not gay; they may be libidinous or desperate or lonely or whatever, but they're not gay. Disagree with me if you need to, but I'm telling you that's the truth.

There is about the same percentage of the world's population that is homosexual as there has always been (10%), you just hear about it more now than you did in the past, for many reasons, and so it may appear that something strange or unprecedented is happening in society that isn't necessarily happening.

Gay people, as a rule, are not anti-family, or even anti-heterosexual for that matter...they are not against the idea of Adam and Eve and what they represent.

Every gay person knows that, were it not for heterosexual procreation, none of us, straight or gay, would be here! Straight people will always be straight and gay people will always be gay.

Period.

I know that statement usually opens up endless arguments on the subject, but so be it.

Sooner or later, people are just going to have to realize and admit that no one is making this stuff up. If someone says they're gay...they're gay! They didn't choose their orientation any more than any heterosexual chose his or her orientation.

Why would a man like me say it if it weren't true?

I would have absolutely nothing to gain by saying it, especially at this stage in my life; as I said before, I wasn't outed by anyone, didn't have a scandal, and at the time of writing this chapter, I am not even in a relationship and am celibate...and I'm still gay.

Why would a teenager make it up about himself or herself just to be bullied or ostracized...or worse, to have a reason to commit suicide?

The only 'gay agenda' that gay people may have is their desire to have the same civil rights that every other citizen has.

Gay people are not after your children, no matter what the fear preachers tell you to make you afraid for their own control purposes. You should protect your children from *pedophiles,* and pedophilia and homosexuality are two COMPLETELY different things.

The overwhelming majority of child molesters are straight men who desire little girls, and the average gay person is just as horrified and disgusted by child molestation as any heterosexual, American citizen, or Christian. And please don't send me statistics and horror stories about Catholic priests and altar boys; I'm telling you, those men are in another category, entirely.

So relax...Adam and Eve and heterosexuality rock, and gay people don't want to destroy the family or the country or civilization as we know it...and they're not after your children. They just want to be able to live their authentic lives the way that you and everyone else wants to live theirs.

So I hope the next time you hear a guy on Christian TV say 'God didn't make Adam and Steve' you'll think about these words and realize how insensitive, idiotic, and out of touch with reality he sounds.

Now to answer more often-asked questions...

But before I deal with this next one, I need to give it some context.

Earlier in the book when I referred to the 'Adam and Steve' comment, I mentioned another often-said phrase that I find equally offensive:

Love the sinner, hate the sin.

Truth be told, I actually think this is the most offensive one...in fact, it's the deadliest...because it sounds so nice and fair and progressive and "Christian," but at the heart of it is a cynical, condescending and smugly self-righteous sentiment that literally sends shivers up my spine.

It's the poisoned apple of homophobic slurs.

More than anything else, it's a lie.

I've seen from my own experience that, typically, the "Christians" who say "Love the sinner, hate the sin" in an attempt to sound benevolent yet uncompromisingly moral, not only hate the 'sin' as they judge it, they actually loathe the 'sinner'...and making this smarmy, phony statement is an unctuous way for them to camouflage their true feelings about it.

Their attempt at reconciling the Christ-delivered mandate to love everyone unconditionally with their actual contempt for homosexuals, exhibits the very kind of hypocrisy that Jesus continually attacked with a vengeance.

The absurdity of 'Love the sinner, hate the sin' reminds me of the scores and scores of letters I've received from those fluent in Christian-ese who begin their pompous missives with the statement, "It's not my place to judge you," and then set out to write three to five pages of nothing but judgment on me!

It's as if saying, "It's not my place to judge you" is the disclaimer that gives them carte blanche to tear into you and say anything they want to say...like when someone begins a conversation by saying, "Now, I'm just saying this in love...."

You know full well, if you've ever been on the receiving end of that opening line, that the words you hear spoken after that are generally anything but loving!

Here's a thought: if it's not your place to judge, then don't even write the letter!

And if you're saying something in love, you don't even have to qualify that it's said in love...love bears fruit of itself! Margaret Thatcher said, "Being powerful is like being a lady. If you have to tell people you are, you aren't"; in the same way, if you have to tell someone that love is your motivation for doing or saying something, it's the clearest indication that nothing could be further from the truth.

Some of those same people have written in those same letters, "Your personal life is between you and God," to which I also say, "EXACTLY! Then why not just let God and me deal with it?"

Anyway, this brings me to the question I get asked all the time:

QUESTION #7: Is homosexuality a sin?

ANSWER #7: No way to answer that because it's not a valid question. Sexual orientation is not what you do, it's who you are!

The guy who always says 'Love the sinner, hate the sin' is the worst kind of homophobic bigot, in my opinion, because he hides his prejudice inside polite statements like that in an attempt to deflect his real motives and true feelings.

He reduces homosexual orientation to merely a sex act, usually between men—one that he doesn't understand or finds repulsive—but let me re-affirm that there is no specific definition of gay sex, even though a lot of straight people think that there is. Just as there is no specific sex act that makes someone heterosexual, there is no sex act that determines whether or not a person is gay. Not all gay people express themselves sexually in the same way (just like with straight people), and it goes without saying that gay men do not and could not have the same sexual expression as gay women.

Being gay is NOT about how someone has sex but about WHO that person is attracted to (more about that in the next chapter).

In fact, as I've already said, if a person is gay and never has sex, they're still gay!

If a gay man spends years going through 'treatments' to cure himself and he learns to control his behavior...if he subjects himself to cultural expectations and is pressured into marrying a woman...he's still gay! The same is true for lesbians.

They are the way that they are...the way that God created them...it's how they're wired.

When homophobes, especially the religious ones, make it all about sex or a particular sex act with which they are pre-occupied, their tactics are transparent.

Many of the letters I've received from those who have quoted the most Bible verses to me are actually quite obscene; in fact, in most cases, the more Bible references they include in their letter, the more graphic and distasteful their language usually becomes about what they imagine intimacy between gay people to be.

The tactic of creating 'the other,' through demeaning people by associating them with abhorrent behavior, is what the men who support the "Kill the Gays" bill in Uganda use.

I won't even mention them by name, but these guys are reprehensible because they lump all gay people into one bizarre sexual category and convince the public that all gay people are extreme and dangerous perverts.

It was the strategy so effectively used to turn a frustrated people against a disenfranchised minority in Germany many years ago.

When you make homosexuality only about the 'sin,' as some call it, you purposely marginalize gays.

At this point you may be asking, *"Where's the GOOD NEWS in all this, especially in a book that's supposed to be about GOOD NEWS?"*

Well, sometimes you have to expose the bad news for what it is so that you can exalt the GOOD NEWS, so again, please bear with me through this.

But a little education is in order here.

First of all, not all gay men engage in the same sexual practices.

I'm trying not to be indelicate here, but I know and have counseled with a very large number of homosexual men who do not enjoy what many straight people assume is the only definition of homosexuality.

As I said, not all homosexuals are men, so what a straight person may think of as the definition of homosexuality probably doesn't even apply to women.

And I don't want to shock anyone, but I've been counseling with people long enough to know that many straight people do everything that gay people can do sexually, which brings me to the next question:

QUESTION #8: Does gay sex cause HIV/AIDS?

ANSWER #8: Absolutely not! No sex act 'causes' HIV/ AIDS; the virus can be transmitted through a number of sexual practices, just like it can be transmitted through blood transfusions and the sharing of hypodermic needles, neither of which has anything whatsoever to do with sex.

QUESTION #9: Then why is HIV/AIDS such an epidemic in the gay community?

ANSWER #9: Because, typically, gay men, especially young, single gay men, are statistically more sexually active with a larger variety of partners than are other groups.

I'm neither defending nor explaining that last answer.

It is what it is.

But that does not mean that any specific sex act *causes* HIV/AIDS.

And finally...

QUESTION # 10: Is HIV/AIDS the judgment of God on homo-sexuals?

ANSWER #10: It is not.
I feel ridiculous even including that last question, because any intelligent person knows that couldn't possibly be true, if for no other reason than there were no cases of HIV/AIDS before 1981 and homosexuality has been a reality in the world since at least the beginning of recorded history.

I mean, if it was God's judgment on the gays, it sure took Him a long time to figure out what to do to punish them.

OK, enough of this for now.

Thanks for reading with an open mind.

CHAPTER FOURTEEN

"I Always Feel Like Somebody's Watching Me"

Abner! Abner! Come look!
– Gladys Kravitz

Funny how confirmation works.

I'm a little more than halfway through writing the book at this point and the last few days, as I've been looking over the previous chapters, the thought has occurred to me more than once that maybe I don't need to deal with some of the things about which I've written.

Maybe some of what I've said isn't even necessary.

Maybe I'm repeating myself.

Maybe I'm overstating the obvious about Biblical interpretation, especially as it relates to sexual orientation.

I mean...this is the twenty-first century, right?

People know all this stuff already, right?

Maybe I should just take out that last chapter, altogether.

Maybe I sound too cynical, especially for a book that's supposed to be about GOOD NEWS.

And then....just when I was about to start second-guessing the whole project...bam!...an all-out assault from a "Christian"... someone who believes that the Holy Spirit sent them to confront and rebuke me about pretty much everything this book is about (and they didn't even know I was writing it).

They came from out of nowhere...came when I least expected it, from a place that surprised me...caught me totally off-guard... just a casual social setting in which I thought I was simply relaxing with some friends.

We were laughing and talking and having a great time, and then...pow!...it was an ambush...totally unprovoked...we weren't talking about God or the Bible or gay issues...we weren't even talking about me or my story...just chilling and having a good time...and there it came...wham!...it was an attack...and the speech was classic...a religious diatribe filled with homophobic slurs, misinterpreted and misquoted Scriptures taken out of context, and loads of misinformation about 'the gay lifestyle'... and then a personal rebuke from this person I had never even met before...

So I just went with *"a soft answer turns away wrath"* and let them spew their venom all over me until they felt that God was satisfied, and then they left...but not until they re-affirmed to me that they were sent there by God to do God's work.

Then, as they went away, content and self-satisfied with their own righteous indignation, we went on with the conversation and the relaxing and the chilling.

I've heard all of what they said before, so it was kind of like water off a duck's back.

But the good that came out of it was that it triggered a change in my thought patterns of the last several days.

In an instant I went from, *"Maybe I shouldn't be writing all of this stuff"* to *"Wow, do I ever need to be writing all of this stuff!"*

The person who accosted me in the name of the Lord only confirmed to me that every word of this book is necessary and right on time...they convinced me in their own way that I'm doing exactly what I'm supposed to do.

So thank you, angry religious person whom I'd never met and will probably never see again. Thanks for giving me the clarity and confidence to keep writing and not change a single word of what has already been put down in words. Thanks for the energy boost; you were just what I needed!

So...where was I?

Oh, yeah.

During my fifteen minutes of fame, I was treated very kindly by the mainstream press: *ABC News, CNN (Don Lemon), The Joy Behar Show, NPR, The Huffington Post, The New York Times, People Magazine, Creative Loafing, Perez Hilton, The View, The Gayle King Show*, and others were very gracious and fair in their coverage of everything concerning my coming out, and I greatly appreciated it.

Not that it matters now, but there were some who said I was enjoying the press coverage a little too much and was playing to the media, but what they didn't know is that I turned down many more interviews than I accepted; a producer who makes movies for HBO approached me about doing a biopic (which I turned down), and even though we signed contracts for a reality show, that project has not been picked up by any network as of yet, and I am totally fine with that.

The stuff that was written about me was something over which I had no control and I didn't ask for any of it.

Whatever about all that, but the biggest issue was, of course, the "Christian" press.

Ah, the Christian press...where do I start?

I have, for the most part, kept silent about this, but I feel free to address it now.

At the time of this writing, all you have to do is Google my name and you'll find an abundance of Christian gay watchdog groups who have had a field day with discussing me, dissecting every word of my coming out message (one guy had so much time on his hands that he created an entire eight-part series off of that one message) and showing their general obsession with me and with people like me.

And there are hundreds of comments from "Christians" on these blogs and under the YouTube videos that have to do with my story. Some of these "Christians" would try to post as many as twenty times a day on my blog (all anonymously, of course).

Just think of how many homeless people they could have fed (something that Jesus actually talked about) in the time it took to post twenty homophobic rants a day.

It's hard for me to take the Christian gay watchdog sites seriously as being anything that actually resembles being Christian, because there is nothing at all about Jesus on their blogs and websites (at least nothing that I've seen)...maybe because Jesus was completely silent on the subject of sexual orientation, as we've already discussed.

All you will find on these websites is blatant intolerance, homophobia and hate speech.

Just scroll down and read the comments on their blogs, or the comments posted under some of the YouTube clips of me, and you'll see what I mean. They and their followers are so gossipy, judgmental, petty, Pharisaical, fundamentalist, closed-minded, vulgar, and just downright mean-spirited, that they compromise any moral authority they might otherwise have, in my opinion.

As I said, Jesus didn't say a word about homosexuality, but he said A WHOLE LOT about love (*this is the greatest commandment, by this shall all men know that you're my disciples,* etc.).

Just read some of the "Christian" anti-gay blogs and tell me if you read anything that sounds even vaguely loving written in them.

What I would say to them if I could (which I can't, because they have no willingness to listen to anyone but themselves) is: Why do you care so much?

Why do you have an opinion about anything I do or say at all?

I think you guys take the Scriptures out of context for your own agendas and preach what Paul called "another Gospel" and yet I would never be arrogant enough to tell you what to preach or not to preach, or set up a blog just to discuss you.

I'm sure they believe that they have a prophetic mandate to expose false teachers like they believe me to be.

I could argue from the Scriptures that the role of a prophet in the New Testament is quite different than that of the Old Testament prophets who announced destruction on unrepentant cities, but I really don't think that's the point.

I think it's a lot more superficial than that.

I think it's this: with so many voices out there today to compete with for an audience on Christian TV and radio, and especially on the internet, you have to say something different and loud to be heard...and this is something that's not limited to ministers ranting about the gays...I'm including all the ministries that take it on themselves to tell everyone else who is wrong or un-Scriptural or immoral or heretical or errant in their theology.

I understand them in a way because they really think they know everything, and I can relate to that...I used to know everything, too! (see Introduction)

Back in the day, I wasn't as downright mean as the "Christian" homophobes are, but I definitely was self-righteous like them, so I get that part. It's awesome to really believe that you are right and that everyone else is wrong.

But it seems to me that those who want to be heard, but really have nothing to say, have no alternative but to tell you what's wrong with what everyone else is saying...kind of like they're the bottom-feeders of the religious fundamentalist ministry food-chain...scavengers who make a lot of hay out of telling you what's wrong with everyone else because that's all the material they have to work with.

And people like me have provided them with a lot to write and talk about, so I guess I would also say to them, "You're welcome!"

But, all sarcasm aside, I also want to say *"Father, forgive them, for they know not what they do."* The very religious are often also very unhappy; it's really hard to *Behold the Lamb of God who takes away the sin of the world,* when all you can see is the 'sin of the world' in everyone else.

At this point, the thought may have crossed your mind that if I'm so magnanimous and forgiving of my critics and attackers, then why even talk about them (the Christian press, et al) at all?

I think it's a valid question...one that I've asked myself more than a few times.

In fact, I'm constantly examining my motives for everything that I say (write) and do.

And I am also of the persuasion that if you are intentionally provocative, then you forfeit the right to moan and whine when people are provoked by what you say and do...it comes with the territory.

But I would like to point out that Jesus, while being the perfect example of one Who constantly turned the other cheek and even laid down His own life, also never missed an opportunity to call out those who opposed Him, especially in the religious community.

I don't think the two concepts are mutually exclusive; in other words, I forgive all who have said really horrible things to and about me concerning my telling the truth about my sexual orientation, but I also think that it's my responsibility to tell it like it is and shine a light on their hypocrisy and ignorance.

Jesus called the Pharisees *"snakes and vipers"* and *"white-washed sepulchers filled with dead men's bones,"* but He also said to them (nearly in the same breath) *"The Kingdom of God is within you."*

My examining the things in this chapter has as much to do with trying to figure out why people are so preoccupied with the personal lives of other people as it has to do with issues of sexual orientation in general.

Why can't Christians just let other Christians *work out their own salvation with fear and trembling?*

I graduated from a well-known Liberal Arts/Bible College—a university that was birthed out of one of the largest Pentecostal denominations in the world—and, in all the years since I left there, I basically never heard from any of my class-mates regarding anything I did or said in over three decades.

I have maintained a handful of relationships from there in the thirty-plus years since I finished my course of studies, but no one I went to school with attended either of my weddings, never commented when I had children or when I left the denomination...no one acknowledged that I started a church which became one of the largest churches founded or pastored by anyone who graduated from there...certainly the largest of anyone I was friends with. Since 1985, only three people I went to school with ever stopped by to see any of the buildings we built when Church In The Now was at the height of its success. I mean, with the exception of one friend who was my roommate my freshman year that I have maintained a close relationship with, I pretty much have never heard from anyone about anything in my life since 1980 when I graduated.

But, boy, when I came out they were all over me and were suddenly more than chatty and extremely opinionated—hostile e-mails, open rebukes on the social networks, lengthy discussions about me on their personal pages—suddenly, after thirty-two years of total silence, they all decided to talk...to me and about me...a lot.

Again, I'm not complaining about it so much as I'm trying to understand it.

If I had been caught in a sex scandal with a woman, would I have heard from the other alumni about it?

If I had left the ministry, would they have an opinion about it?

Would they have been so vocal about anything else?

Why did it take me coming out to finally get some reaction out of them...some acknowledgment of anything about my life?

To all of my classmates who openly attacked me when I came out, I would say, "Hey, guys; where have you been all my adult life and when did it start mattering so much to you what I did?"

A very well-known, super-rich pastor of an Atlanta mega-church preached about me to his enormous congregation and said that I was *"a sign of the times"*...evidence that *"the very elect would be deceived in the last days."*

Having absolutely no idea of what people like me have struggled with their entire life, he dismissed it as me being unable to ignore my perverted 'feelings' even though I've been married twice and have lived my entire adult life in opposition to my nature.

Wow; thanks for the love, Pastor.

What I would say to him if I could, would be: According to your eschatology (which I don't embrace) shouldn't you be happy that I'm a "sign of the times"?

Aren't you supposed to *"comfort one another with these words"* and *"lift up your heads, because your redemption draws near?"*

Instead of judging me, you should be praying for me and should also be excited that Jesus is about to return!

And for the people who have told me anonymously online that I'm going to hell, I would say, "Well, then...shouldn't that take care of it? If I'm going to hell anyway, there's really no purpose in writing pages and pages about me, is there?

Why not just let God take care of me, or deal with me as He sees fit in eternity?

And to the pastors who have 'demanded' online that I step down from the pulpit I would say, "Who do you think you are? God called me to the ministry and only God could remove me from it. I probably disagree with nearly everything you preach, but would never have the audacity to tell you to step down. Jesus is Lord, not me."

The main thing about the Christian anti-gay websites, however, is that I think there is a bigger problem with them, which is that many of them are quite obviously dealing with their own sexual conflict in being so obsessed with someone else's sexuality.

I have read about tests that have been done on these 'God hates fags' kind of Bible-thumpers who are the first to be physically aroused by gay pornography when exposed to it, and it doesn't surprise me.

Time and time again I am reminded of Shakespeare's immortal line, *"Methinks thou dost protest too much!"* (a misquoted line from Hamlet which actually reads, *"The lady doth protest too much, methinks"*) when I hear these guys preach their homophobic sermons or read their homophobic blogs.

However it's quoted or misquoted, the meaning of it is that when someone insists so passionately about something not being true or untrue, then people suspect just the opposite of what that person is saying.

To make my point, it would be too easy to mention people here like John Paulk (no relation to my uncle), Lonnie Latham, George Alan Rekers, or even Ted Haggard...just a few examples of men who have been outspoken opponents of gay rights or have preached condemnation to people with same-sex attraction, who have been caught in gay sex scandals.

There are so many instances of that kind of thing happening that there is even an entire website devoted to exposing these guys called, *Evangelicals Who Hate Gay People but Love Gay Sex.*

To further make my point, I could refer to the brilliant HBO documentary *Outrage*, which tells story after story of politicians who, in the spirit of Roy Cohn (the man who worked for Joseph McCarthy in the 50's and exposed people for being gay but was gay himself and later died of AIDS) and J. Edgar Hoover, have made the lives of gay people miserable by their policies and unfair laws, but have been outed in even more gay sex scandals themselves.

There is definitely a pattern with these guys.

The ones who yell the loudest about it are generally the ones dealing the most with their own inner sexual conflicts.

I would never out anyone myself, but I could even add some personal confirmation to this by saying that after coming out I have been privately contacted by men who say they have had sexual relationships with some of the very people who have been the most critical of me and have said some of the most hurtful things about me for admitting to my sexual orientation.

Some of them are people I know personally, but I choose to take the high road and not expose them for their hypocrisy... just trying to understand it...

What they say and do is between them and God, and God alone is my vindicator, so I refuse to take these matters into my own hands.

I only mentioned the names of some people here because what happened to them is public record. I'm not exposing anyone or revealing new information in citing them as references.

I've been asked about Haggard and Bishop Eddie Long in nearly every interview I've done since coming out, and I've chosen to keep my opinions about them to myself. I did sort of discuss

Haggard briefly on the *Joy Behar Show,* but that was more in the vein of stating my disbelief in the effectiveness of any kind of conversion therapy.

Anyway, the bottom line is that no weapon formed against me will prosper, the gifts and calling of God are without repentance (irrevocable), and I have favor with God and man.

The GOOD NEWS is that the haters online have given me a lot of great publicity that has ultimately attracted many new people to my ministry (Thanks, guys!)...

And the GOOD NEWS is also that, at the end of the day, we will all stand before the Judgment Seat of Christ and give an account of and for our own lives...not the lives of others...and the GOOD NEWS is that we know that He is good and merciful and kind to all...it is not His will that any should perish!
So again I say, Father forgive them all.

And forgive me, too.

And help me understand why things are like they are.

And help me to believe that things can change for the better... that people can love one another unconditionally... that they (we) can learn to mind their (our) own business...to *"owe no man anything but to love him"*...and whatever they (we) don't understand about one another, they (we) can just leave in the hands of God...that more than anything else we can all just Behold the Lamb of God Who takes away the sin of the world.

Period.

The idea of living in that kind of world sounds like GOOD NEWS to me!

CHAPTER FIFTEEN

"What's Love Got To Do With It?"

To the pure in heart, all things are pure...
(Titus 1:15 -- NLT)

Well, it's not a question, really...

Just something that I need to make clear...

...and it's this...

Sexual orientation is not just about sex!

When I was in the middle of experiencing my fifteen minutes of post-coming-out media attention, I would get hit with a lot of questions about sex in many interviews...particularly questions about my own experience in that area...and I always tried to move the conversation in a different direction when that would happen.

I suppose it's understandable that I would get those kinds of questions, but I just hated to have to answer them.

It's not that I had anything to hide about my sex-life...as I've already said in this book, enough time has now passed that it should be clear that I was not outed by anyone...my coming out was not a publicity-driven attempt to get in front of an about-to-be-revealed sex scandal, make the story my own and protect my public image, as many haters in the blogosphere speculated.

Even after my divorce, I could have just not said the whole truth about myself and could have saved myself a lot of pain, hassle and trouble. Even though, in that case, many would probably be suspicious of the real reason for the break-up, I could have just done what many closeted public figures do...could have maintained a secret relationship or had secret sexual encounters and could have kept the public persona somewhat protected.

Actor Raymond Burr (*Perry Mason, Ironside*), for example, managed to keep his male partner out of sight for decades (the man he considered to be his husband) and his fans were none the wiser. He's just one of many, many famous gay people who have kept their private reality totally private. Many high profile people live that way today in Washington, and even in liberal Hollywood, in order to preserve everything they've worked for.

And it's certainly not that I'm squeamish about talking about sex.

Anyone who knows me knows that I don't have trouble talking about anything...and I mean *anything*!

In fact, I freely and openly discuss things about politics, racism, sexism, religious intolerance, homophobia, ignorance, phoniness in the ministry, hypocrisy and the gimmicks that many preachers use to be successful quite frequently in the pulpit.

The words "I can't believe you actually said that out loud!" are words I hear quite often.

I even publicly speak so candidly about my own faults, mistakes and idiosyncrasies that it's a wonder anyone ever even gossips about me. That's why I can say with confidence that you shouldn't believe everything you may hear or read about me...if something's true, I probably would have already told everybody about it, even if I have sworn to my own hurt to do so. If I haven't said anything about it, it most likely didn't happen, because I live my life (especially now) as an open book.

If there had been a sex scandal that prompted me to come out, I would have been the one to go public with it. It's just too exhausting trying to hide something that's inevitably going to be revealed about you. I'd rather just let everyone hear it from me *("Confess your faults one to another...")* and let the chips fall where they may.

In other words, I just don't need "don't ask, don't tell"...

No, the reason I don't like to talk about the sexual aspect of being gay is because too many straight people ignorantly assume that's what it's all about.

I reiterate, being gay is not a choice, nor is it a sexual fetish, or even a particular kind of behavior for that matter.

When you make it just about the physical, you marginalize those with same-sex attraction, overlooking important aspects of their lives such as love, romance, affection, commitment, relationship, partnership, family, paternal/maternal instincts, sharing a life together, dealing with loneliness, community, growing old with someone, longevity, owning property together, having/adopting/raising children, and so on.

In my congregation (both locations) are same-sex couples who have faithfully been in monogamous relationships for 5, 10, 15, 20, 25 years or more...a couple in my Midtown Atlanta congregation just celebrated their 37th anniversary (they met in college and have never dated anyone else, male or female). I got a beautiful letter recently from two men who have been together for 41 years...and, in states where gay marriage is now legal, you see some couples who have been together for more than 50 years who are just now able to have their long relationships recognized and acknowledged in that way.

These are people who often work together, own homes together, own businesses together, go to church together, take care of one another in sickness and in health, take care of one another's parents in their old age, have children together, and don't cheat on one another...

In a word, these are people who LOVE one another!

Whether or not they have the insurance or legal benefits or any of the other perks that straight married people often take for granted, they are in real and committed RELATIONSHIPS...

...and they're not just having sex all the time!

Again, sexual orientation is not about WHAT YOU DO...it's about WHO YOU ARE!

I was gay long before I ever had sex with anyone, male or female, and if I were to remain celibate for the rest of my life, I would still be gay, because that's how I'm wired (oriented)!

Again, straight people don't become heterosexual upon having a sexual experience with the opposite sex...they just are and always have been straight.

A heterosexual man or woman could go to his or her grave a virgin and still be straight, because that's their orientation.

Same thing for gay people...it's who they are, not what they do...

No one chooses heterosexuality.

No one chooses homosexuality.
You just are what you are, regardless of what you decide to do (or not do) about it.

If you never act on your sexual impulses, you still are either gay or straight (some include bi-sexual here, even though I have my own opinions about that subject, which I will save for later)... you just are who and what you are.

Straight people can disagree and argue about that fact ad infinitum, but it doesn't change the reality of it.

You Can't Be Serious!

Most of the deluge of hate mail that I was getting daily when I first came out has pretty much died off now...as I've already said, the letters I got from "Christians" were so mean and nasty and hateful that they were nearly comical...like it was a practical joke. I don't think I could have gotten nastier stuff written to me if I had murdered my parents. For some reason, the "Christians" just really can't stand for some people to be themselves, especially gay people (even though Jesus was silent on the subject...and, again, I know I've said that before, but it bears repeating)...

Anyway, one typical line of thinking that was in many of those letters was the comparison of homosexuality to bestiality and pedophilia. Lots of people said to me, "If you say you were born with this orientation, then what's the difference with people who say they were born a pedophile or that it's in their nature to have sex with animals? We don't allow those people to do what they feel like doing, so why should we allow homosexuals (usually they insert the word 'sodomites' here) to live open lives?"

Please allow me to answer this incredibly insulting question...

It's such a stupid and mean-spirited argument that I shouldn't even dignify it with an answer, but I'll do it anyway...

The simple answer is that human beings cannot have consensual, committed relationships with animals, and adults cannot and should not have consensual relationships with children!

If gay people were incapable of love, relationship or commitment, these people might nearly have a point...but, as I have said, it's not just about who you have sex with, it's about who you are attracted to...who you love...I could even run the risk of making stereotypes by saying that orientation often determines a person's taste in music or movies or fashion. I know, in my own case, that there are certain types of entertainment (Broadway, for example) that I have always loved and followed and that have nothing whatsoever to do with my sex-life. I'm not saying all gay men know and like show tunes, but a lot of them do, including me. I'm not saying all lesbians like football and shop at Home Depot, but a lot of them do. Without trying to box anyone into a label, I'm just trying to make the point that orientation is a much bigger thing to deal with than with whom a person sleeps.

Another thing you hear from these people is that gay people, especially the ones who want to get married to each other, are changing the definition of marriage that we have observed from the beginning of time...and that's just not true. I've already discussed this in the book, but even the men in the Bible were nearly all polygamists and had harems. Even the concept of marrying for love is a relatively new and modern idea...and it wasn't that many years ago that it was illegal for people of different races to get married, and back then the haters used the same arguments against mixed marriages.

Just because you don't understand or can't empathize with the way someone else sees the world, doesn't mean you have the right to condemn it.

This Is Personal

I don't know why, exactly, but of anything I've written here so far, this next part is the hardest for me to put into words.

I've been putting it off for weeks...every time I sit down to finish this chapter, I just can't seem to do it...can't seem to deal with the memory of this...and I hit a wall and have to put the book away and not think about any of it for a while.

It's not writer's block. It's something more complex than that.

No doubt, some of you will be incapable of understanding why this is so hard for me to talk about, especially since I've already touched on so many controversial aspects of my life, theology and sexuality in the previous chapters.

But I'm not afraid of controversy; it's never been a problem for me.

I was considered controversial in the religious world long before I came out, so I'm very familiar with the territory. And holding a mirror up to the ugliness and ignorance of what often comes out of the religious mindset of so many is actually very empowering for me on a personal level.

Nothing that I've written about so far comes from a victim mentality, because I don't have one.

I am at peace with God and with myself.

But I have to talk about this to fully explain why this chapter is so important...to address why I refuse to let those who don't understand what it means to have same-sex attraction reduce it to being just about sex...or to label it as a perversion or something unnatural just because it seems unnatural to them.

As I've already said, same-sex attraction isn't unnatural to those who have it.

Anyway, let me just go ahead and put it out there and then I'll explain why it's so hard to talk about.

Basically, it's this: when I was around 10 or 11 years old, I fell deeply in love with a boy who was about a year older than me whose family lived a couple of doors down from where we lived at the time.

You may be thinking, "That's it? That's the thing that's so hard to talk about?"

Please don't judge what I just said until you hear me out.

First of all, he never knew it and doesn't know it until this day. With the exception of a short, generic e-mail that I sent to him a couple of years ago, I have had no contact with him for over 40 years and, from what I know of his life as an adult, he is a straight man who is married and has a family.

One of my hesitations in writing about this is that I didn't want him to somehow hear about my talking about him or get a copy of the book and be embarrassed by what I'm saying or to become angry with me about it. Some straight men have killed gay men for saying similar things about them. There's even a legal defense for the murder of gay people called *The Gay Panic Defense* in which a straight man is able to claim that he totally freaked out because a gay man told him that he loved him or made a pass at him and, as a result, killed the gay man during a bout of reactionary, responsive, temporary insanity.

Amazingly, this defense often holds up in court and, in many cases, straight people are regularly exonerated for the assault or murder of gay people.

I don't think he would want to kill me for what I'm about to say, but honestly, these days gay people can't be too careful.

In the world of Facebook and other social networks, word can travel very fast and it's entirely possible that he may read this or at least hear about it.

In the event that he does, let me again make it clear that he is not a gay man and he and I never had any kind of physical relationship whatsoever...which is precisely the reason I need to include this in this chapter.

Well, let me qualify that...I did receive a harmless bear hug/ wrestling hold from him as we and some other kids from the neighborhood were running through a garden hose sprinkler one summer afternoon a lifetime ago...it was basic horseplay between boys that I'm quite certain meant absolutely nothing to him...I, on the other hand, can very vividly remember the sensation of his wet skin next to mine and the way it made me feel. I'm not trying to be provocative here...just trying to make a point...and the point of saying it is that I had never before felt what I felt when that happened and I never once in my life felt anything that nearly equaled it from a female...

"But you were just a boy!" you may be saying to yourself. "This memory should be a non-issue in your life...a typical instance of normal, adolescent male bonding that happens to most people."

My response to that is, "No...a thousand times, no!"

And here's why...

I'm not talking about the physical sensations that any boy begins to feel around that age as he awakens to his sexuality (regardless of his preference)...I only mentioned the day in the sprinklers because it so clearly stands out in my mind and reveals something about who I was at the time...and about feelings that there is no way I could have chosen to have...

It's just a memory...like the memory a straight man has of what he felt...about what awakened within him...the first time he kissed a girl...

But what I felt that summer day when he touched me is nearly a side issue because I'm talking about something quite different from a sensual experience.

I'm talking about love.

"But you were just a child," you may say... "you were too young to even know what love is...the most you could call that is puppy love."

To that I say that puppy love is very real to the puppy and, as much as a kid of that age can or could love someone, I promise you I was in love with him.

I know what it is to have a crush on someone.

This was different.

Let me say here that this kind of experience is real for a lot of kids, both straight and gay.

That's why an adult should never trivialize or dismiss young love, especially a first love.

If you've ever done any research on the teen suicide epidemic, you probably can appreciate what a big deal this is for some young people.

I know it was for me.

It was the first time I can ever remember feeling love for someone...and it was real...and somewhere in the mind of my inner child it is as real to me today as it ever was.

Let me also interject that the middle school years for kids are sometimes really, really hard for them...much harder, in fact, than all the high school years put together. I know middle school was a constant trial for all four of my kids...really did a number on them for different reasons and, as I remember, they all had some miserable experiences during those years... but they loved and did well in high school and are all now well-adjusted adults.

This would be a good time for me to encourage those of you with middle school-aged kids (6th, 7th and 8th grade) to cut them some extra slack right now...they may currently be going through very traumatic things that you know nothing about.

My parents certainly were unaware of what I was going through at the time.

In fact, one reason the feelings I had at that age for this boy were so significant for me is that it was a very rough season in my life, one in which I was emotionally vulnerable because of the nature of my relationship with my father.

He and I have made peace now, and I intend to say nothing in this book about him that I will regret later, but suffice it to say that my father had made it abundantly clear to me, even at that young age, that sissies were unacceptable and that homosexuality (as I understood it at the time) would never, ever be tolerated or even understood by him.

I believe there is a statute of limitations on how long you can be angry with your parents for whatever reasons, and I have certainly put away childish things when it comes to my attitude toward both of mine.

The man my father has become in his senior years is quite enlightened and tolerant, and he has even paid a great price among his own friends and in his own denomination for not publicly renouncing me when I came out. His refusal to disown me (which resulted in him having to surrender his ministry credentials to the denomination) was an act of redemption on his part that deeply healed something in me that very much needed healing.

That being said, I can't even begin to imagine what the man my dad was back then would have done to me if I had even hinted to him that I was in love with a boy!

I literally shudder to think about it...

There is no possible way that I would have ever even come close to discussing with either of my parents (or anyone else, for that matter) the feelings I was dealing with at the time.

"OK, we get it...you really liked a boy when you were a kid; what's the big deal?" you may be thinking.

Let me see if I can make you understand why I'm even talking about this.

Last week I was reading a typical hate-letter from a Christian who took it upon himself to inform me (once again) that the Bible said it's an abomination for a man to lie with a man as with a woman (by the way, the ONLY time people ever quote Leviticus or any of Moses' 613 laws is pretty much exclusively for gay-bashing, but I digress)...anyway, as I read his typical, crude expression of disgust for what he perceives that I like and do sexually, my mind went back to a certain afternoon in my boyhood when I lived in that house two doors down from the person I felt at the time was the love of my life.

And that's why I even brought this up at all.

When people say that being gay is a choice or that it's just about sex or about giving place in your life to a sexual aberration, I can't help but remember what young love felt like to me...love that wasn't a choice...love that was entirely non-sexual, but was love, nonetheless...and I realize once again how incredibly ignorant some people can be.

Let me say here that I am fully aware that straight people certainly know what unrequited love is all about...anyone, straight or gay, can fall in love with the wrong person... someone who doesn't love them back or is unavailable to them...someone who belongs to someone else. The heart wants what it wants, and love has a mind of its own and often love hurts...a lot...in fact, probably everyone has experienced this on some level.

But when a gay person falls in love with a straight person, there's a whole other dimension of pain involved. In these cases, rejection is almost guaranteed, but it's not just your standard rejection...not just the rite of passage of a broken heart that every person experiences at one time or another.

Ellen Degeneres once eloquently described the isolation that closeted gay kids experience, and I had never thought of this until she said it, but I agree with it. Her point was that even if a kid who is part of a minority experiences prejudice or rejection, they at least have other people in their world who are like them and can understand what they're going through. For example, if an African-American kid gets called the "N" word on the playground, he or she at least has a home, a family, a community of other African-Americans whom he or she can talk to about it...like-minded people who can provide empathy and support.

But when a gay kid who can't tell the truth about himself or herself experiences prejudice or rejection, they can't talk to anyone about it. In most cases, they are strangers in their own homes. They don't even know anyone who is like them... I certainly didn't. Even those closest to them can't possibly empathize with what they may be going through, even though they may experience it repeatedly.

Anyway, back to that afternoon many years ago.

It was a Wednesday, and we had church every Wednesday night, so I was supposed to be doing my homework...was supposed to finish it before church that night.

Church was mandatory...attendance was never one time optional.

I not only went to church every Wednesday night of my life (besides Sundays and the other days of the week for whatever reason), I usually had to sing or play my saxophone in the service or attend a youth meeting...one way or the other, I always participated in church.

So I remember that I was lying across my bed that afternoon, supposedly working on a social studies or math assignment (but most probably I was drawing pictures or writing the name of the boy I loved over and over again)...anyway, at one point in the attempt at engaging in something that resembled homework, I looked out my window and saw something that literally took my breath away for a few seconds.

I saw him walking down the street with the little girl who lived in the house between our two houses.

In my memory, they were holding hands...I don't know for sure...but I remember they were definitely laughing and having a good time...I remember looking at him as he looked at her and recognizing that he had never looked at me that way...and in that instant it dawned on me that he would never in a million years look at me that way...he certainly would never walk down the street, laughing and holding my hand... that's for sure.

I'm not a good enough writer to explain to you what happened to me in that moment.

Even as I write about it now, I know it probably doesn't seem like that big a deal...I just don't know how to describe the pain that my 11 year old heart felt upon seeing them together that day.

I'm feeling it even as I write about it as if it just happened, but I still don't have the language to convey what I experienced standing there at my bedroom window.

It was more than just the realization that he liked girls...I'm sure I already knew that, but I had never seen it manifested before.

If I had been a girl who was in love with him, I could have tried to compete with her for his attention.

But I wasn't a girl.

I was a boy.

A boy who liked boys.

A boy who liked boys who didn't like boys back, and never would.

And this is why I won't let people who don't know what they're talking about get by with saying that sexual orientation is exclusively about sex.

That day I watched the boy I loved walking with a girl... I watched them for as long as I could until they disappeared over a hill in the subdivision...

And then I collapsed in a heap on the floor in the way that a marionette puppet does when its strings are cut, and just began to sob.

I sobbed the deepest sobs I ever remember sobbing in my life up until that point.

I sobbed as quietly as I could so that my parents wouldn't hear me, because if they heard they would naturally want to know what in the world was wrong and there was no possible way that I could tell them.

I sobbed on that hardwood floor in my bedroom until it felt like my guts were going to come out.

I sobbed because I didn't know what to do with the feelings I had for him.

I sobbed because I knew I could never tell him about it.

There's no way he could ever understand, and he certainly didn't feel the same way about me.

If I told him, he might hate me and never speak to me again. He might call me a fag.

I'd been called that before on the playground at school because I didn't know how to play ball...I already knew what that felt like...I remembered the day in third grade when they threw me a football at recess and (I swear) I had never even seen one before...had no idea what to do with it. My dad never watched football, and I had no brothers and no male playmates to speak of, so football wasn't even in my consciousness...

But this was about more than not being able to play sports... the bottom line is that even if he understood my love for him, it wouldn't make him stop liking girls...it certainly wouldn't make him love me...

I sobbed because I couldn't tell anyone about it.

I sobbed because even at that young age, I knew that I would never feel that way about a girl.

My parents would never accept it.

I couldn't even talk to God about it because He would just send me to hell for loving a boy, so I avoided the subject with Him, altogether.

Bottom line, the jarring reality check that I got in that instant—about who I was...about who I loved...about every-thing that was wrong with my young life—just came crashing in on me all at once...it was a moment of truth, but not the kind of truth that sets you free...all it did for me was make me want to die.

I don't know how long I lay on that floor and cried...I just cried until there weren't anymore tears.

By then it was time for church and on the way there, when my mom noticed my swollen, red eyes and demanded an explanation, I came up with some lie...I don't remember what I told her...whatever it was she didn't buy it, but the service was about to start and she had to play the organ, so the subject was tabled...

Remember when you were a kid and you cried really hard and then got the hiccups from it? Well, I played the sax that night with a serious case of the hiccups...with deep gaps in my breathing from having cried so hard...it was an ordeal, but I got through it.

Then, somehow, after church we just never discussed it and I went to bed and it never came up again.

He and I remained friends after that, but it became increasingly hard for me to be around him because my feelings for him were so intense. I started having bouts of depression, but I disguised them as much as I could.

My extended family still chides me to this day about what a moody kid I was...about how I always look so gloomy in the family reunion home movies that were taken during that time period.

When they say it, I think, "You have no idea..."

A few months later we moved away and I never saw him again.

About a year after that I felt the call of God into the ministry and started channeling all my energy into trying to serve Him...and into trying with all my might to not be gay.

That's when I entered the "on-fire-for-Jesus phase" that I talked about in the beginning of the book.

Throughout my life, I fell in love with a lot of my straight friends, and they never knew it.

I just learned to deal with it.

No one ever suspected because I was always dating girls.

I slept in beds with friends of mine that I was very attracted to over the years and practiced enormous amounts of self-control, because they never knew it, either.

But that first one hurt.

Big time.

I would be embarrassed for him or anyone else to actually know how many times over the years I have driven over to that town and have gone to that neighborhood and sat in my car in front of his house hoping that I would see him...hoping that if I did, I would somehow find the nerve to tell him how I felt...not that I thought I could convert him (because that can't be done, I don't care who tells you that it can)...but because thought at one time, especially during the years I was still trying to be delivered from homosexuality, that talking to him about it would somehow be a key to set me free.

This went on for decades, even after I was married and had kids of my own.

Even after I knew for sure that he didn't even live there anymore, I still drove over there a lot. I can't explain why...just trying to make sense of my life, I guess...but every time I went, I cried again.

It's amazing how much you can cry over someone in your life who never even knows about it.

Anyway, I finally stopped driving over there a couple of years ago...right about the time I came out; in fact, I don't think I've gone there once since I came out.

Once, I looked up his new address and drove by where he lived at the time...I thought I saw him coming out of the house and panicked and sped off...I don't know why...I just did...it sounds irrational, I know, but it is what it is (or was what it was)...

I hesitate to even admit to all of this because I know it makes me sound like a stalker or a crazy person, but I need to drive home the point about orientation that I'm trying to make...

So, to those who say that orientation is a choice or to those who think it's just about sex, I say, "Tell it to that broken-hearted kid lying on that floor crying his eyes out all those years ago...and to a million other broken-hearted gay kids (who have never had sex with anyone) who experience the same thing every day"...

You have absolutely no clue how misguided your opinions are.

Love is real...

...even if you don't understand it.

> *He who answers a matter before he hears the facts—*
> *it is folly and shame to him.*
>
> (Proverb 18:13 – AMP)

In other words, don't attempt to speak with authority about something you can't possibly understand.

That's what love has to do with it.

OK, I'm ready to move on now...

CHAPTER SIXTEEN

"Your Own Personal Jesus"

Don't set yourself up as a judge who takes the liberty of casually condemning others, or even as a critic who thinks that he or she has the right to criticize them, because when you do that, you set a universal law into motion that will inevitably bring negative things back into your own life. In other words, don't judge so that you may not be judged and criticized and condemned yourselves. For in direct proportion to your judgment, criticism and condemnation of others, you will be personally judged and criticized and condemned. It's just the way the law works. And in accordance with the measure you use to deal out to others...whatever you may deal out...it will be dealt out again to you. You define the terms of your own life in this sense. And why do you fixate on the very small particle...the tiny speck of sawdust...that is in your brother's eye, while you are completely unaware of and oblivious to the huge beam of timber that is in your own eye? Or how can you obsessively say to your brother, 'Let me try to get that tiny, superficial splinter that I'm preoccupied with out of your eye,' when all the while there is the beam of timber that is obvious to everyone but you lodged in your own eye? Don't be such a clueless hypocrite! Work on dislodging that beam of timber from your own eye first, because until you can completely remove such glaring, personal obstructions, you're frankly not qualified to take on the responsibility of extracting anything at all from your brother's eye, no matter how big or how small."

(Matthew 7:1-5 – GITN)

Wow...where was the GOOD NEWS in *that* chapter?

After reading the second half of it, you may be asking that question.

It's a legitimate one.

But for me, telling that story still falls under the category of my sharing GOOD NEWS with you, for the simple reason that I can even talk about it and still be OK.

I hope I've already made this clear in the book so far, but, in case I haven't, allow me to reiterate something...

There is nothing that I have shared in these pages that comes from a "victim" mentality.

On the contrary...I actually feel empowered by sharing the painful stuff.

Like the boy David running toward the giant, my being able to discuss these things out in the open takes away the sting of them...it makes me feel fearless because I know in my heart that there's absolutely nothing that I'm afraid to talk about.

Someone recently said to me, "I hate that you have to write about all the religious haters and share some of the mean-spirited things they have written and/or said about you or to you in your book!"

I quickly assured them that I don't share the negative things to sound whiny or victimized or even to complain about them.

The only reason I even talk about that kind of stuff at all is so I can hold up a mirror to the ugliness of religious intolerance (of any kind) and show it...expose it...for what it really is.

I feel like it's my duty.

To whom much has been given, much is required.

I don't worry about the homophobes and modern-day Pharisees and their fundamentalist rhetoric.

Their problem with me is their problem, not mine.

But I was thinking about this yesterday as I sat down to write this chapter.

I was thinking about the audacity and arrogance of religious people who feel it is their God-given right and responsibility to correct everyone and to make sure everyone else stays in line.

Religious people are generally so loud and nosy...so involved in and committed to expressing their opinions about everyone and everything.

When I started writing this book I was 53 (now about to turn 54)...I am a grandfather and have been preaching for 40 years...I have been a successful pastor...more successful than most, in fact.

I am re-stating these things here to make the point that I could play the "Elder" card and be loud and opinionated about everyone in the Church-world with whom I disagree. I could feel justified in telling everyone who I thought was right and who I thought was wrong... about who I thought was "of God."

And sometimes I do, on occasion, say something in a sermon about a public religious figure if I think it's pertinent to the point I'm making at the time.

Yet it would never cross my mind to fire off letters or to get my thoughts onto blogs or on the Facebook pages of others whom I don't even know, to confront or rebuke them about their theology or their life, or anything else for that matter.

Sometimes I read the rebukes that people send me and think, "Who do you think you are?"

I'm sure I've already said all this at some point in the book (probably more than once), but yesterday as I was thinking about the attitude of the very religious, because of something someone had posted on my FB page, I began to write this down in response...

And, because It's good and pleasant for brethren to confront the loudmouths (resist the devil and he will flee from you...), I thought I would include it here in this chapter...

CREDO
by Jim Swilley

1. **I AM NOT YOUR CREATOR**: I choose to believe that it was God, not I, who created you in His image (Genesis 1:26), so I will respect and always try to recognize whatever parts of His DNA are evident in your makeup, whether or not you ever conform to the image of who I think you should or shouldn't be. Your relationship with Him is something personal...something that is between you and Him alone... and so I not only realize that I will never fully understand it, I can also rest in the knowledge that I don't have to. Your relationship with your God is something that I'm not even required to have an opinion about, because God is God and I completely trust Him as your Creator!

2. **I AM NOT YOUR SAVIOR**: I choose to always remember that it was Jesus, not I, who chose you in Him before the foundation of the world, that you should be holy and without blame before Him in love (Ephesians 1:4). I also choose to remember that it was Jesus alone, not I, who died on the cross for you. I took no stripes on my back for you, and so I am unqualified to make a judgment call on your relationship with the One who did. I choose to remember that it is He, not I, who now ever lives to make

intercession for you in order to "save you to the uttermost" (Hebrews 7:25). Your relationship with Jesus Christ is something personal...something that is between you and Him alone...so I have no choice but to accept it as it is as you work out *your* own salvation "with fear and trembling"! (Philippians 2:12)

3. **I AM NOT YOUR LORD**: If you say that you have confessed Jesus Christ as your Lord, then I have no choice but to believe you and to accept that as a fact, even if my experience with Him is quite different from yours. You do not have to answer to me for your life, because you did not confess me as Lord over it. And if you never confess Jesus as Lord in this lifetime according to my definition and understanding of it, I *still* choose to believe that every knee will ultimately bow and every tongue will, indeed, confess to that fact, and so I believe that will include you, according to my understanding of it. In the meantime, my only responsibility to you is to love you! (Romans 13:8)

4. **I AM NOT YOUR HOLY SPIRIT**: I will remember to trust the work of the Spirit in your life and will recognize that it is He, not I, who began a good work in you, and so it is He who will continue to perform that good work until the Day of the Lord (Philippians 1:6). I have neither the ability nor the responsibility to convict you of what I may perceive to be sin in your life. Whatever needs to be added or taken away from you is strictly in the hands of The Helper, and I will not be arrogant enough to assume that I could or should do what only He is qualified or supposed to do in you, for you, or through you!

5. **I AM NOT YOUR JUDGE**: However you interpret the Scriptures is something that I choose to respect, even if your interpretation is quite different from mine. And if you don't believe the Scriptures, or even acknowledge them, I will still consider it my responsibility to be a "living epistle" before you, regardless of what you do or don't believe

(2 Corinthians 3:3). You do not owe me any explanation for your world-view or theology (or lack thereof), and I will not use certain Scriptures about *"exhortation"* or *"provoking one another to good works"* or being a *"fruit inspector"* to impose my opinions on you, manipulate you, or to defend my desire to control you in any way. I will not religiously hide self-serving motives behind certain verses of Scripture taken out of context to defend my desire to mind your business. My only request is that you will give me the same consideration.

6. **I AM NOT YOUR PASTOR**: I am not your Pastor, unless you tell me that God alone has led you to that conclusion... and if that is, in fact, the case, it must only be because He has placed you in the Church *"as it has pleased Him"* (1 Corinthians 12:18) and because my gift makes room for me in your life. And if I am, indeed, your Pastor, I am only a shepherd who works for the Chief Shepherd to *lead* (not drive) the flock...I will not be a *"Lord over God's heritage"* (1 Peter 5:3), but will aspire to be one who "rules with liberty." And if I do ever have a personal "word" for you, it will not come from my own opinion of you or of what you do, but from the Holy Spirit...and even then that word should be judged, as should all prophecy. I understand that as your Spiritual Leader I must *"give an account for your soul"* (Hebrews 13:17), but as a general rule, your personal life is none of my business. Period.

7. **I AM NOTHING MORE THAN YOUR FRIEND AND BROTHER:** I will not judge you and will, to the best of my ability, love you unconditionally as you are continually conformed to His image in the way that is unique to you. In so doing, I am making the effort to fulfill the **Golden Rule**, doing unto you *as I would have you do unto me.* I don't need you to be wrong for me to believe that I'm right. Please recognize that God is my Creator, not you... that Jesus Christ is my Savior and Lord, not you...that the Holy Spirit is working in my life according to His good

pleasure, not you...and that only God can judge me, not you. You are not even required to have an opinion about me or anything that I do or say and, unless you ask me for my opinion, I will not impose mine upon you in any way. I will respect your right to live your life as you see fit and to interpret the Scriptures as you believe the Holy Spirit leads you to do, without any interruption, intervention, opinion or commentary from me, whatsoever. I will allow God alone to be God in your life, as you allow Him alone to be God in my life. And even if I am your pastor or leader or teacher or spouse or partner or father or son or fill any other role in your life, I will still only want God's best for you and will pray that His will, not mine, will always be done in your life on earth as it is in heaven!

This is my pledge to you...

જ

I hope these words get the point across.

What I'm talking about here is bigger than whatever has happened in my personal life.

It's bigger than the issue of homophobia.

It's bigger than the issue of dealing with fundamentalism.

What I'm talking about is what's wrong with Christianity and religion in general today...about why there are so many atheists in the world...about why with every generation the church is becoming less and less relevant to society.

People are tired of other people simply refusing to allow other people to live their own lives.

Go back and read the Gospels and look for the real Jesus.

That Jesus wasn't a jerk.

Now that's GOOD NEWS!

CHAPTER SEVENTEEN

"We Shall Overcome"

Slaves, obey your earthly masters in everything...
(Colossians 3:22 – NIV)

It's always so interesting to me to see the way things turn out when you're in the flow of your gift.

I should have finished this book months ago but, in my defense, it's been quite an eventful year so far and I've had a lot going on in my life to distract me from writing, to say the least.

I won't go into detail, but trust me when I say that I've had more than enough on my plate of late, and the resulting circumstances have demanded that I fill so many different roles that the 'author' one has necessarily been put on the back burner again and again.

As a result, the book has pretty much evolved through 'fits and starts,' as they say, and at least twice I decided to scrap it altogether, as I've already revealed in a previous chapter.

I have entertained the thought at certain times that, because it is taking so long to get it done, maybe this was just supposed to be nothing more than my own (unpublished) personal journal, written solely for my own catharsis.

At this point in my journey, most of the deluge of hate-mail and general antagonism from the religious community that I was once dealing with has pretty much died down (or died off), the homophobia-induced exodus from my church is apparently over, and I'm personally the happiest and most internally peaceful that I've been since I can remember. I say that to explain that much of the personal impetus for writing this to begin with is now a moot point.

And everyone tells me I'm much nicer now than I used to be... whatever that's about...so I have thought on occasion that perhaps the writing had served its purpose.

To give you some perspective on the creative time-span, there have not only been major shifts and changes in my public life/ministry during the course of this writing, there has also been significant transition in my personal life. I was single when I started writing this, and then I was in a relationship for about a year, and then I was single for about seven or eight months, and now (at the time of writing this chapter) I'm about two months into another (much better) relationship.

As a result of all that has been going on with me and with the church, I have actually gone for months without writing a single thing for the book.

And when you work like that it's easy to lose momentum...and perspective...on your project.

But every time I start to think that maybe the book isn't for publication, something seems to happen that serves as a cosmic kick in the pants and gets me back into the game.

When I began forming the ideas and themes for the book, I wrote out a Table of Contents as an outline of all the chapters that would cover everything I wanted to talk about here. One of the chapters was to be about racial issues as they pertain to the subject matter contained in these pages (by the way, I haven't forgotten that the book is about GOOD NEWS!), so I wrote out the title for Chapter Seventeen: *"We Shall Overcome."*

I've been staring at that title for months, with no real inspiration to attach a chapter to it, and had decided as of last week to go ahead and publish it as is, with only sixteen chapters (the original plan was/is for twenty-one). But that was last week.

This week there is suddenly an abundance of inspiration and a million things to say in this chapter.

Of course I won't get to all one million things, but now I at least know why I've waited until now to write this chapter.

My steps are definitely ordered.

I think one reason I've put off writing this chapter for so long is that there could definitely be some question, even on my part, as to whether or not I should even touch this subject.

In the Preface, I referred to the standard (and I consider sage) advice given to all authors: WRITE WHAT YOU KNOW, and because I believe in that premise, I don't want to get down to the end of this writing and start delving into topics that are beyond my grasp or my ability to understand or relate to with any kind of real empathy.

But, at the same time, I do want to say everything that I had originally intended to while I have this opportunity.

Specifically, I want to deal with the subject of race and homophobia before I send the manuscript off to be printed for public consumption.

Even more specifically, I want to deal with both the real and perceived homophobia of the African-American community and the "Black Church" in particular.

I grew up in a very multicultural and racially diverse world and am quite comfortable in that environment, so it's no surprise that the church I founded took on some of my personality, including my attitude toward diversity. Our congregation has been racially diverse from its inception in the spring of 1985 and, at this point in our history, the demographic of the church body (at least at the original location in Conyers) is predominantly African-American.

One question that I have been asked quite frequently and consistently in the months following my coming out (especially from people of color that are in contact with me from literally all over the world) is: "Did all the black people leave your church when you told them you were gay?"

Obviously (and thankfully) the answer to that question is, "No, they did not."

Timing Is Everything

It certainly will be interesting in future months and years to read this chapter in light of the way all of this will eventually play out, but at the time of this writing it is an election year and President Barack Obama is running for his second term in office.

As I said, I had pretty much decided not to write this chapter and just go ahead and send this off to be published (mainly because I'm so behind schedule in getting it done), but just as I was about to put the finishing touches to the manuscript, the President made his public statement endorsing the rights of gay Americans to be married, which subsequently set off a firestorm in the Black Church.

I saw this as a confirmation that I should go ahead and talk about this, even though I have been told in no uncertain terms by some in the African-American community that, as a white man, I have no business and/or authority to discuss this at all.

But I disagree.

I am a minister. I am an American. I am gay. I am a voter. I am a taxpayer. I am pastor to a lot of black people. I honor and respect the Black Church and its important place in American life and unique role in the shaping of American history, particularly in the area of the Civil Rights movement. And I love and pray regularly for my President...even drove all the way to Washington D.C. just to stand out in the freezing cold to attend his inauguration.

Not only is it my right to talk about this, I believe it is my responsibility.

As I write this, as recently as yesterday the NAACP stepped up and officially made the same endorsement for the rights of gay people as did the President a few days earlier, which has brought about even more conflict within the Black Church.

Their explanation for their reason in doing so at this time was that their position was and is basically based on Dr. King's assertion that "a threat to justice anywhere is a threat to just everywhere"...that Civil Rights is really about human rights across the board...that to not make a statement in regards to gay rights, especially now that the President has taken an official stand on gay marriage, would essentially compromise their moral authority as a Civil Rights organization.

Coretta Scott King once said,

"Gay and lesbian people have families, and their families should have legal protection, whether by marriage or civil union. A constitutional amendment banning same-sex marriages is a form of gay-bashing and it would do nothing at all to protect traditional marriages."

On another occasion she said,

"I still hear people say that I should not be talking about the rights of lesbian and gay people and I should stick to the issue of racial justice. But I hasten to remind them that Martin Luther King, Jr. said, 'Injustice anywhere is a threat to justice everywhere.' I appeal to everyone who believes in Martin Luther King, Jr.'s dream to make room at the table of brother- and sisterhood for lesbian and gay people."

But over the last few days, the news and YouTube have been filled with clips of sermons from black pastors, demonstrating the backlash (some call it "blacklash") to the President's comments. One prominent African-American pastor of a large and historic church stood in his pulpit last Sunday, officially denouncing Obama, whom he had previously supported, claiming that the President's support of equal rights for gay Americans was a destructive threat to America equivalent to the terrorist attacks on 9/11. (A white pastor of a large church also told his white congregation the same day that all the gays and lesbians should be quarantined and surrounded by an electric fence until they all died off, but this is about the Black Church, so I won't mention that guy...or the white pastor who, a few days earlier, told his North Carolina congregation that they should vote against Obama, and if any of their sons were sissies they should punch them out...but I digress.)

Makes you wonder if anyone in the Church still just simply preaches the Gospel of Jesus Christ!

I've heard some leaders claim that for gay people to try to relate their struggle in any way to that of African-Americans in this country is not only a travesty—an insult to those who gave their lives for the Civil Rights movement—but that it is also 'pimping out' the movement because sexual orientation is, in their view, a choice, and skin color is not.

Some years ago, Elder Bernice King, a minister and the daughter of Dr. King, spoke at an anti-gay rights rally sponsored by Bishop Eddie Long's ministry when she was still employed by his church. In her speech that day she said,

"I know in my sanctified soul that my daddy didn't take a bullet for same-sex marriage."

But her mother, who often spoke at Gay Pride events, was quoted as saying,

"My husband, Martin Luther King, Jr., once said, 'We are all tied together in a single garment of destiny...an inescapable network of mutuality...I can never be what I ought to be until you are allowed to be what you ought to be.' Therefore, I appeal to everyone who believes in Martin Luther King, Jr.'s dream to make room at the table of brotherhood and sisterhood for lesbian and gay people. Gays and lesbians stood up for civil rights in Montgomery and Selma, AL, in Albany, GA and St. Augustine, FL., and many other campaigns of the Civil Rights Movement. Many of these courageous men and women were fighting for my freedom at a time when they could find few voices for their own, and I salute their contributions."

It goes without saying that I have great respect and reverence for the iconic widow of Dr. King. Not only did she carry on his mission and live out the essence of his message more than anyone else has before or since, but as an Atlanta native and child of the '60s (and a gay man), I feel very connected to her legacy of courage. Much of the Black Church publicly turned on her when she stood up for gay rights, including many in her own family, but she never apologized for it or backed down at all for her stance.

That's why I stood for four hours in the rain outside Ebenezer Baptist Church just to pass by her open casket when she died and then was privileged to be able to attend (with my son, Judah) her historic, six-hour funeral at New Birth Missionary Baptist the next day.

She was an amazing woman who deeply understood what her husband lived and preached.

Doing the right thing isn't easy and it often comes with a great price. I vividly remember passing by the "Christian" protesters outside her funeral as we entered the church who held up banners and signs saying "No fags in Dr. King's dream!" and "She's in hell!"

"What's Goin' On?"

Much has been studied and written about why particular oppressed people groups often eventually oppress other people groups. It's a phenomenon that is difficult to understand. Sociologically and anthropologically, this often-repeated historic reality is closely related on a psychological level to the reason that sexually or physically abused children often grow up to be sexual and physical abusers themselves.

It has never made sense to me.

I would think if I had been abused in such a way as a child, that I would absolutely reject any impulse I might have to pass on the abuse to another generation. I certainly know that, in my own case, I disciplined my own children quite differently from the way I was disciplined as a child (not that I was abused... just saying that I didn't do it at all the way my parents did), so it would stand to reason to me that victims of abuse would be anything but abusers!

But clearly...and sadly...that's not the case.

Nearly every case of child abuse reveals a continuation of a trend in a dysfunctional family

In the same way, I would think that any group that had been oppressed would, if anything, be nothing at all but champions of ending oppression for other groups.

Thankfully, Dr. King understood that principle—and he certainly was not the only one in the African-American community who did—it's just unfortunate that so many leaders in the Black Church apparently have such limited vision in this area.

That's why it was so encouraging to me to see the NAACP take the stand that it did this week.

It's only right.

And when it comes to the Black Church and the stereotype of its gay intolerance, I can only marvel that some men and women who are supposed to be theologians don't realize that the same Bible they use to bash gay people was also used to promote and defend slavery in this country!

I won't go into a study of it here (I'll save it for my next book), but suffice it to say that even in the New Testament, slavery is strongly supported. It certainly was supported by Paul, who clearly believed that some people were born to nobility and some to servitude. Even with his great revelation of the Christ, he was a product of his times and its ignorance and prejudices.

As I've said before, it's why the Scriptures must be rightly divided.

Do a little study of the abolitionist movement in this country and you'll see how much history is repeating itself with the spirit of the way people use the Bible to argue both sides of gay rights.

There was a time in this country that the Jewish community and African-American community were very emotionally connected and mutually supportive, and now they are not so much.

This is an extremely simplistic explanation of the present gulf between those two communities, but, as I understand and perceive it on a very basic level, it boils down to an impasse in the argument of who had it the worst as a people, historically, bringing up the much-debated and unanswerable question: which is more horrible, the Holocaust or American Slavery?

I've been involved in those types of conversations in which someone inevitably brings up the plight of the Native Americans and the Trail of Tears, and no one ever wins the argument because all of it is horrible.

Man's inhumanity to man never makes sense and can't be rationalized.

But let's say for argument's sake that people of color had it the worst, a premise with which I have no dispute... slavery...the Middle Passage...Jim Crow laws...lynching... modern forms of racism and injustice for minorities...all of it...

To the African-American community at large, I say: if indeed your experience has been the worst...the most inhumane...the most unjust...shouldn't that make you even more compassionate and sensitive to the pain of all other disenfranchised and oppressed people?

Martin Luther King and his wife, Coretta, certainly believed that it did...listen again to his description of 'The Beloved Community' and tell me that everyone isn't included in that vision!

And to the Black Clergy which has been very outspoken in a negative way about me, I say, please rightly divide the Scriptures and use them only to share the GOOD NEWS...the GOOD NEWS of liberty and love and acceptance and understanding and empathy and being salt and light...be the liberators that you were called to be and learn from your own experience that the letter kills, but the Spirit gives life!

Please...if Jesus didn't talk about it, then don't worry about it... in a word, just preach the GOOD NEWS...love God...love others!

Can't we all just get along?

CHAPTER EIGHTEEN

"There's A New World Coming"

And that's just the beginning: After that I will pour out my Spirit on every kind of people: Your sons will prophesy, also your daughters. Your old men will dream, your young men will see visions.

(Joel 2:28 – The Message)

As I've been saying from the beginning of the book, it's all about GOOD NEWS!

GOOD NEWS for the future.

GOOD NEWS for you!

As a seer and visionary, I am very excited about where I see the world heading. Oh, I know about all the negative things... about all the suffering and strife in the world...about all of our problems that should have been resolved some time ago.

But I also see many good things on the horizon...changes— sometimes little changes, but changes nonetheless—changes that continue to move us in the right direction.

Having been a pastor for so long (and the son and grandson of pastors), I have seen, first hand, many different types of human suffering over the entire course of my life. I am very aware that violence and hatred and prejudice and intolerance and injustice are rampant in many parts of the world and also in our own backyard...and I'm also fully aware that religion has had a lot to do with many of those things.

But at this point in my life and ministry, I find that I am considerably and consistently more and more optimistic and less and less pessimistic in my world-view and, in large part, that is due to my connection with so many young, and young-thinking, people in my life. The kids in my life, including my own awesome kids, continue to inspire hope for the future within me.

I talk to so many young people who seem to have such a firm grasp on what is really important in life...they are enlightened and unencumbered with many of the old ideas that have kept previous generations (including my own) in a certain kind of intellectual and spiritual darkness. They appear to have religion and faith in much better perspective than many of their predecessors and elders do and instinctively possess an understanding of the importance of love and acceptance in the world.

In a word, the young people that I know are much more connected to seeing the big picture, and that makes me hopeful that my kids and grandkids will live in a better world than the one in which I have lived.

A Personal Note To Young People

You have your whole life ahead of you...so much to live for...so much for which to look forward!

Be who you are.

Be who you were meant to be, even if it takes you a lifetime to figure out who that person is. One thing is for sure...no one else can figure that out for you...it's your journey...your discovery... your path.

You are the hero of your own story...the star of your own movie... the lead singer in your own band!

The world is not perfect, but it's a wonderful place to live and there are so many adventures awaiting you...make the decision not to miss any of them.

Believe in God...in something (Someone) bigger than you... and give your life to loving and serving Him. Don't worry about trying to be religious...the God that you know in your heart of hearts is the right One...follow Him...don't let anyone tell you otherwise.

Believe in the Gospel...in the True Gospel...the Gospel of God... the Gospel that is only GOOD NEWS...the simple Gospel that very basically consists of two foundational ideas: Love God and Love others (as you love yourself)...living selfishly will never bring you happiness...love is always the answer.

If anyone tells you the Gospel is more complicated than that, don't believe them.

The Gospel of Jesus Christ is the GOOD NEWS, made up of those two ideas only.

Learn to listen to your inner voice, and trust it.

Do what is right for you.

Believe that God has a plan for your life and do everything you can to connect with that plan.

Be happy.

Life is too short to live any other way.

Believe that all things are possible.

Believe in yourself.

Maximize your potential in every way possible.

Learn as much as you can...never stop!

Travel...see as much of the world as you can...if more people traveled and met other kinds of people, there would be less prejudice and intolerance in the world.

Think outside the box.

Recognize injustice when you see it, and speak out against it.

Help people.

Always be a part of the solution, never a part of the problem.

Learn to forgive, including forgiving yourself...don't waste your life on bitterness.

Worship God!

Listen to smart people...let them mentor you.

Learn from your mistakes.

Follow your bliss.

Tell the truth.

Celebrate life!

The future belongs to you!

A Message To Gay Teens

Dear One,

You're beautiful, just as you are...and God loves you just the way you are!

NEVER let anyone convince you otherwise!

You are *"fearfully and wonderfully made"* (which is just an old-fashioned way of saying that God created you perfectly, in every way)!

You are not broken.

You are not inferior.

You are not weird.

You are not a pervert.

You're not abnormal.

You are not less than.

You are not an abomination.

You are not going to hell.

You don't need to be 'fixed.'

In a word, you're AWESOME.

And you're in good company...

Many important historical figures were gay...

Plato...Alexander the Great...Pope Julius II, to name a few...

So were some of the greatest artists who ever lived, such as...

Leonardo da Vinci and Michelangelo...

...as well as some of the most important composers and musicians of all time, such as Tchaikovsky, Leonard Bernstein and Katharine Lee Bates (the woman who wrote 'America the Beautiful')...

And some of our most important writers were gay...people like Walt Whitman, Thomas Mann and James Baldwin...

I could also mention sports figures like Billie Jean King or actors like Raymond Burr...or religious icons such as King James of England (yes, that one!)...

The list of important historical gay figures goes on and on, but the point of bringing them up is to reinforce the truth that these people undeniably made huge contributions to our culture and society...

...and the world is waiting for you to make your own unique contribution to it!

I hope that you have the love, understanding and support of your family, especially your parents, but even if you don't because of your orientation, let me encourage you to still love and be who you are.

As a gay man, a minister, and a father (and grandfather) myself, allow me to speak to you as a father...always be yourself and love, accept and respect yourself as the wonderful creation that God brought into this world...your life is very important and God has a purpose for it!

If your parents support and accept you as you are, then count your blessings...you have amazing parents!

If they don't, then pray the prayer of Jesus for them, Who said, *"Father, forgive them, for they know not what they do,"* and move past it as best you can...don't hate them...hatred will never bring anything good into your life.

They may feel that it is their responsibility to try to change you (even though you are who you are, and always will be!).

They may have limited understanding of the Bible and think that preaching it to you will change you (even though God knew exactly who you were when He created you!).

They may feel that your orientation is their 'fault' and are dealing with a lot of unnecessary guilt over it (even though the overwhelming evidence points to the fact that you were born the way you are!).

They may feel sadness at the idea of you not ever getting married or giving them grandchildren (which, in this day and age, is becoming less and less of an issue for gay people!).

They may be afraid that if you're gay you won't have a good life (which you have to show them is a fallacy by living a good life!).

They may simply be afraid of what they don't understand (in which case, help them understand, if you can and if they're open to it!).

They may be thinking and feeling all of the above.

Just have compassion on them and show them that you are happy with yourself. The more the people in your life see that you're OK with you, the more they will relax and just let you be yourself. You know the truth about what it means to have same-sex attraction...that it's not a choice (no matter how much straight people constantly insist that it is)...so in this case you have to be the bigger person (which isn't easy when you're the kid and they're the adult(s)!...but it is what it is...so get it together and live your life; and if they accept you, great... and if they don't, find people who will and love and honor your parents for the simple fact that they are your parents. We all want the approval of our parents, but sometimes we just have to take what we can get and know that God (our heavenly Parent) approves of us.

And don't let anyone use a few Scriptures *taken out of context* to confuse you or clobber you with. Do your homework...find out what the Bible actually says (and doesn't say). Never let anyone use religion to manipulate you or try to control you. Knowledge is power!

And finally, NEVER, EVER, EVER let some ignorant, homo-phobic bully rob you of any part of your life!

NEVER, EVER, EVER do anything to hurt yourself, no matter how bad the bullying is!

Push back!

Speak up!

Say something!

Get some help!

Tell somebody what's going on!

Don't shut up until you get the help you need!

Make some noise!

Make a difference!

Bullies are cowards who are drawn to your insecurities like sharks are drawn to blood!

The more comfortable you become with yourself, the more powerful you become and the less likely you will be a target for homophobes.

You have a responsibility to live the life you were meant to live, so never even consider the possibility of ending that life! If you do, you will break all of our hearts and you will miss out on so much! Don't do something crazy in a moment of despair! There's always hope!

> *If God be for us, who can be against us?!*
> (Romans 8:31)

You have a responsibility...a responsibility to help create a new world...one in which bullying is simply a thing of the past.

No matter how overwhelmed or scared you may feel, you have to live! You have to be strong! You have to rise above it!

If you let the bullies win, then all those gay kids (and any other kids who are 'different' in any way) who will come along in the future will have to deal with the same nonsense!

Don't just survive for yourself...do it for those kids!

Don't ask for trouble, but at the same time, don't forget that this is your world, too, and no one has the right to tell you how you should live in it!

God believes in you.

I believe in you.

And there's a whole world of people out there who will believe in you, too...don't allow some bonehead to steal your world... your life...

Believe in yourself!

Be the thermostat of your life, not the thermometer...

You can determine the life that you will live...

Your best days are ahead of you...

There really is a new world coming, one in which people can live their own authentic lives in peace, without the threat of someone always trying to control or change them.

Now that's GOOD NEWS!

I speak a blessing over you and over your family...and over your future...I pray for good friends...a good support system for you...for your protection...for favor with God and man...for your well-being...for your happiness...that love will be in your life... for healthy relationships...that you will continue to walk in truth and that that truth will continue to make you free...that God will make Himself real to you and that you will know and believe from the bottom of your heart that He is love and that He is good!

> *I know what I'm doing. I have it all planned out—*
> *plans to take care of you, not abandon you, plans to*
> *give you the future you hope for.*
> (Jeremiah 29:11 – The Message)

CHAPTER NINETEEN

"What The World Needs Now Is Love"

My beloved friends, let us continue to love each other since love comes from God. Everyone who loves is born of God and experiences a relationship with God. The person who refuses to love doesn't know the first thing about God, because God is love—so you can't know him if you don't love.

(I John 4:7, 8 – The Message)

God is Love. Period.

It's quite probable that I've already referenced this Scripture in the same translation somewhere in the book in some previous chapter.

If so, so be it.

If not, then it's about time I talked about it.

I think this particular passage is so important—so central to what the Gospel of Christ is really all about—that if I had included it in every chapter of the book it would not have been too much.

Reading it every day...perhaps every hour...would be beneficial and worthwhile for all of us.

One of my favorite songs of all time is the Hal David/Burt Bacharach classic, *What the World Needs Now*, and, man, if the sentiment of that piece was appropriate in the '60s when they wrote it, it's certainly even more true and pertinent and appropriate NOW!

What the world needs now...more than anything else...is definitely LOVE.

Without a doubt.

The only thing I would add to the song in this day and age would be a verse that proclaimed, WHAT THE CHURCH NEEDS NOW IS LOVE, SWEET LOVE!

I think that it's unfortunate...a travesty really...that these days it seems that Christians, in general, are known for just about anything but for their love (the one thing that Jesus said would prove discipleship!).

In the modern era, as it appears at least in this country, Christians are too often known for their judgmental intolerance, bigotry and prejudice...for being outspoken about all the things that Jesus never said anything about and completely silent on the subjects on which He actually placed importance.

I know I've already said it, but I'll say it again without apology...

God is love.

Period.

End of story.

As I near the end of the book, I hope this one thing will stand out and be remembered—I can't impress it upon my readers too much—if it isn't about love, it isn't about God!

I do want to thank you for taking the time to read my words.

I really appreciate it.

I only ask that you have read it with an open heart and an open mind.

Of course I realize that I can only make the request...and that's exactly what it is...that's all it is...a request.

It's not a demand.

I know that I can't force you to change your mind about anything concerning theology, particularly about certain hot button issues such as eternal punishment...and I can't force you to change your perception of people with same-sex attraction, especially if you've had a negative view of them (us).

But it is my hope and prayer that you will at least sufficiently lay aside any prejudices or preconceived ideas that you may have had to agree with me on this one point: that God is love and that love is the most important thing.

If I can get your agreement on at least that point, then there is definitely value in this volume.

> *Strip yourselves of your former nature [put off and discard your old unrenewed self] which characterized your previous manner of life and becomes corrupt through lusts and desires that spring from delusion; and be CONSTANTLY RENEWED in the spirit of your mind [having a fresh mental and spiritual ATTITUDE]; and put on the new nature (the regenerate self) created in God's image, [Godlike] in true righteousness and holiness.*
> (Ephesians 4:22-24 – AMP)

I love the way The Amplified Bible uses the term *"CONSTANTLY RENEWED in the spirit of your mind"* in this verse...

I think love is the only thing that can enable you to be renewed in such a way.

Love causes your world-view to become 'other-worldly'...

Love enables your attitude to transcend the accepted norm of the natural realm.

Love gives you the strength and clarity to renounce all counter-productive allegiance to cultural tradition.

Love creates a mindset in which you may be born-again so that your thinking is not of this cosmos (world system) any longer... so that you are not obliged to just go along with the crowd in your opinions and perspectives.

Love gives you the power and authority to go against the tide and to swim upstream, if necessary.

Love will make you become willing to re-examine any and all belief(s) that you have in stereotypes and will empower you to deal with each individual in your life, individually, so that you may give them the benefit of the doubt before pre-judging them in any way.

Love will move your attitude in a direction that is predisposed to know people after the Spirit and not after the flesh, in honor of Christ's development of the New Creation Species.

Love will bring perspective to your thinking when it comes to your devotion to ancestry, enabling you to praise your parents (see last chapter), be faithful to your family and honor your heritage...but, at the same time, it will liberate you from feeling bound to be limited to their level of learning or to the laws leading their lifestyle.

Love will give you the courage to reject any latent fear of change that may be resident in your soul and help you keep an open mind and an open heart...and that's very important because, as I've already discussed (see also last chapter), there is a new world coming and only those who live by the law of love will be able to thrive in it.

If you don't agree with me on anything else, at least agree with me on that.

God is love.

Period.

And that's GOOD NEWS!

CHAPTER TWENTY

"Ain't That GOOD NEWS?"

I marvel that you are turning away so soon from Him who called you in the grace of Christ, to a different gospel, which is not another; but there are some who trouble you and want to pervert the gospel of Christ. But even if we, or an angel from heaven, preach any other gospel to you than what we have preached to you, let him be accursed. As we have said before, so now I say again, if anyone preaches any other gospel to you than what you have received, let him be accursed.

(Galatians 1:6-9 – NKJV)

The Gospel is GOOD NEWS. Period.

This verse in Galatians (in which Paul rebukes the church in that city for preaching "a different gospel" or "another gospel") is liberally used in all the 'heresy hunter' books and on all the fundamentalist watchdog websites and blogs (check it out and see for yourself)...

It certainly has been used against me a lot by some of these groups (along with verses about *"wolves in sheep's clothing,"* last days false prophets speaking to people with *"itching ears,"* and those who no longer endure *"sound doctrine"*)...the implication being that I preach something "other" than what Jesus preached.

It doesn't bother me.

If I thought for a minute that I was preaching anything different than the original, organic Gospel of Jesus Christ, I might find it bothersome, worrisome or offensive to be targeted with this verse and others like it.

But because I know the truth and understand the concept of reading the Scriptures IN CONTEXT, it actually amuses me when some religious bigot levels an accusation against me by using this passage, because I actually think that what Paul was talking about here is infinitely more applicable to them than it is to me!

If you understand the purpose and tone of the Epistle to the Galatians, you know that Paul was angry when he wrote it... it's actually his angriest Epistle...and the object of his fury was the fact that these Gentiles, who had never been bound, whatsoever, by the Law of Moses, were leaving the simplicity of GRACE and putting themselves under the bondage of LEGALISM!

As I see it, the "different gospel" that Paul was referencing here was the expressed idea that the true Gospel could be anything other than (or more than) what Jesus actually said that it was... two things: Love God...Love Others...

...and since Paul never talked about any kind of eternal punishment anywhere in his letters, the threat of one being "accursed" here has to refer to curses brought on oneself in this life by not correctly handling the Gospel...by not preaching it in its most simple, most basic form.

I don't know what the manifestation of that kind of curse would be...perhaps it would be different for every individual... but I know I don't want to invite any kind of curse into my life so I plan on always only preaching the Gospel...the Jesus Gospel... the Gospel that is GOOD NEWS. PERIOD!

We already discussed this earlier in the book, but allow me to reiterate here that the true Gospel is what the angels declared to the shepherds when Jesus was born...GOOD TIDINGS of GREAT JOY which shall be to ALL...ALL...ALL PEOPLE!

The question, "If you died tonight, do you know where you would spend eternity?" is not the Gospel.

It's an ultimatum.

GOOD NEWS is just that...news that is GOOD!

Pretty much, any Christian group that disapproves in any way of another Christian group basically believes that group is preaching "a different gospel."

Most denominations are built on the assumption that "we" have the truth and you don't!

"We" preach the truth, but you people are "other" or "different," which is code for "YOU'RE WRONG!"

The word "Pharisee" simply means 'separatist,' and one of the most amazing and confounding things about what the Gospel of the Kingdom that Jesus preached has devolved into (i.e., Christianity), is the fact that there are "Christian Pharisees" (Christian separatists)!

It's the height of perversion!

There are only 27 books in the New Testament and THOUSANDS of Christian denominations!

THOUSANDS of Christians believing and preaching that the other Christians are preaching "a different gospel!"

I personally believe that Paul would be shocked to know that there is so much division in what he referred to (by revelation) as *The Body of Christ* and that so many members of that body use his exhortation (written in a letter to a church in the Asia Minor province of Galatia) to keep each other at bay and to justify their division!

Anyway, I've pretty much covered all of this kind of thing earlier in the book, I just don't want to end the writing without once again reminding everyone who reads this that the Gospel is GOOD NEWS. PERIOD!

A Personal Note

A few days ago, I was doing a radio interview on a program that was discussing President Obama's supportive statement of marriage equality that he had made just a few days earlier.

It was a very good and lively interview and we covered much more than just the subject of marriage equality, but while we were talking, the moderator of the program said, "Bishop Swilley, someone just called in to our switchboard and wanted to inform you of 2 Timothy 4:3, 4."

In case you don't know, the passage says this:

> *For the time will come when they will not endure sound doctrine, but according to their own desires, because they have itching ears, they will heap up for themselves teachers; and they will turn their ears away from the truth, and be turned aside to fables.*
>
> (2 Timothy 4:3, 4 – NKJV)

I knew what the passage said, so I asked him, "What's the question?" to which the moderator asked, "Well, what do you think about that?"

"What do I think about what?" I asked.

"What do you think about preaching sound doctrine?" he said.

I responded, "I'm for it! And I do it! I just don't understand the question, especially in light of what we're discussing."

Of course, I knew the implication that the caller was making... it was an inference that, because I don't fit her idea of what a preacher of sound doctrine is supposed to be like (presumably because of my innate sexual orientation), I owed her an answer concerning Paul's exhortation in a letter to his protégé, Timothy.

So I said, "Well, I believe in the Virgin Birth...I believe in the miracles of Jesus...I believe in His work on the cross...in the power in the blood...in His resurrection...I believe everything in the Apostle's Creed...I certainly believe in Jesus' own definition of the Gospel which is simply LOVE GOD and LOVE OTHERS... I don't know what part of 'sound doctrine' you're asking me about, because I believe and preach all of that."

The moderator (who was not at all being antagonistic...he was actually playing devil's advocate for the sake of his caller) simply said, "And you're gay, right?"

To which I said, "I am...even though it's irrelevant to the issue of whether or not I preach sound doctrine; as I see it in the Scriptures...and the bottom line is this...the Gospel is GOOD NEWS. PERIOD."

Jesus Or Paul?

Where in the Bible do you find the Gospel?

I've been saying for years that to really understand the Bible you have to always remember that it's not a book...that it's a collection of books by many different authors who wrote to different generations of people for very different reasons and is, therefore, loaded with contradictions (which I've already discussed in previous chapters)...but that the truth of it—the 'spirit of the letter' if you will—is inspired and absolute.

Above all else, when we try to define 'The Word of God', we have to keep in mind that the Word became flesh, not pen and paper.

One thing that has really become undeniably obvious to me, especially while writing this book, is the stark differences between the Gospels and the Epistles, particularly Paul's Epistles.

I covered this material in the chapter about Paul ('Listen To What The Man Said'), but I want to revisit it before I close this out.

I've previously mentioned some examples to make this assertion, but I want to point out a bigger issue here which is the general difference of Paul's paradigm from that of Jesus on just about all the major subjects. And this is in no way meant to discredit Paul...I believe that his revelation of the post-resurrection Christ was unparalleled and absolutely flawless, as I've already said.

I just can't be done with this writing until I'm sure I've made this point, because if you don't understand this part, the rest of it might be in vain.

In general, I always say that religion is the enemy, but I need to qualify that statement once again. It's really not religion that ruins peoples lives and causes such division, hatred and intolerance in the world, it's FUNDAMENTALISM...and that's why I want to do everything in my power to deconstruct the world-view of the religious fundamentalist, especially the CHRISTIAN fundamentalist, and do what I can to disarm the haters who continue to use the Bible as a weapon against people they don't like or understand.

Allow me to mention of few of these subjects in an effort to help us all do a better job of 'rightly dividing' the Scriptures instead of 'wrongly connecting' them.

ON SALVATION: Jesus' concept of the way to salvation seemed to be one that is completely connected with how you treat people...the sheep and the goats, according to Him, are separated according to whoever visited the sick and the prisoner, or fed the hungry...*I was hungry and you fed Me*...in the allegory of the rich man and Lazarus, the man is sent to the Greek 'Hades' because he refused to feed a beggar who lived on his doorstep...the harlot is forgiven because she proved she "loved much" by washing Jesus' feet with her hair...Zacchaeus received salvation because he promised to return the money he had stolen from his clients *(This day salvation has come to your house)*.

Paul, on the other hand, seems to have no concept of this. His main emphasis is on how works can't save a person at all. Even when he speaks of the eventual salvation of Israel, he says that *"With the heart man BELIEVES unto righteousness and with the mouth CONFESSION is made unto salvation"*... acts of kindness, benevolence or philanthropy don't seem to be high priority with Paul like they obviously were with Jesus...he also has a tendency to make 'lists' of sins and/or *"works of the flesh"* in his Epistles, and the sin of 'indifference to the poor or disenfranchised' that Jesus made a big deal over doesn't seem to make it into Paul's 'lists'...

ON SPIRITUAL WARFARE: Jesus seems to have had a view of warfare with the forces of darkness as a finished work— *"I saw Satan fall like lightning"...* *"Satan has come to me, but he has nothing in me"*—it's as if once He descended the Mount of Temptation there was no more warfare for Him with Satan... He was simply walking out His dominion in the earth...even when He cast out demons, He did so rather matter-of-factly, in that He would just say something like, *"Shut up and come out of him."* One of His most startling declarations is recorded in John 12 where He announces that the judgment of the world has already come and that *"Now the prince of this world is driven out"*; it's here that He makes the most powerful statement ever about ultimate reconciliation when He says that if He is lifted up (on the cross), He will draw ALL PEOPLE...EVERYONE...unto Himself...

Paul, on the other hand, sort of resurrected the activity of the *"prince of this world"* with his very militant view of our ongoing wrestling with *"principalities, powers, the rulers of the darkness of this world and spiritual wickedness in high places"*...he speaks at length to both the Ephesians and the Corinthians about *"the whole armor of God"* and *"the weapons of our warfare."*

ON RELATIONSHIPS WITH "SINNERS": It goes without saying that Jesus was so public with His fraternization of tax collectors, publicans and the like that He was labeled by the religious hierarchy as 'The Friend of Sinners' (and they didn't mean it in an endearing way)...He even chose a few 'criminals' to be on His staff of Disciples...

But Paul exhorts his readers to *"Come out from among them and touch not the unclean thing"* and *"Be not unequally yoked with unbelievers."*

ON WOMEN: Women were vitally connected to the life and ministry of Jesus, and not just "nice girls": Mary Magdalene, the woman caught in adultery, the harlot who washed His feet with her hair, the woman at the well who had been in so many marriages and was living with a man...all women that would have been ostracized by society...Jesus received and respected (and restored) every one of them...He even publicly called the woman with the issue of blood—who would have been considered a pariah in that culture—"Daughter"; Jesus completely liberated women...

But Paul tells women to be quiet and behave, especially in church, and to not usurp authority over men and to obey their husbands and be in subjection to them and to cover their heads in church to demonstrate their subservience to men.

ON HOMOSEXUALITY: I've already covered this in previous chapters, but the two passages that religious gay-bashers use to clobber people with same-sex attraction more than anything else—even more than the two passages in Leviticus (at least this has been my experience)—are Romans 1 and 1 Corinthians 6, both from letters penned by Paul. The religious "urban legend" that gay people can't go to heaven comes from what Paul wrote to the Corinthian church about who would "inherit the Kingdom"; of course, if you read either of these passages in any kind of context (something that fundamentalists refuse to do), you'll see that Paul's words are regularly misunderstood and misquoted.

But even if they weren't—even if Paul was a homophobic Pharisee who was actually talking about responsible gay people in the modern world being "turned over to a reprobate mind" in Romans 1—the inescapable fact that the gay-bashing fundamentalists can never deny is that Jesus was completely and absolutely silent on the subject.

'Nuff said.

I could go on with other contrasts between the Gospels and the Epistles, but the point is this: Yes, I believe that all Scripture is given by inspiration, but I don't believe that the Scriptures are infallible. Paul had great revelation from the Holy Spirit, but he had enormous influence from Moses, which is why the Scriptures, his letters in particular, must (for the bazillionth time, I say) BE RIGHTLY DIVIDED!

I love and appreciate all the Bible authors, but Jesus Christ is my Lord...

...and the Gospel is GOOD NEWS.

PERIOD.

CHAPTER TWENTY-ONE

"I Will Always Love You"

There's a trick to the "graceful exit." It begins with the vision to recognize when a job, a life stage, or a relationship is over—and let it go. It means leaving what's over without denying its validity or its past importance to our lives. It involves a sense of future, a belief that every exit line is an entry, that we are moving up, rather than out.

— Ellen Goodman

OK…last chapter.

I think I've said everything I wanted to say about everything… at least for now.

Thanks, again, for reading.

I do, however, want to take care of a few loose ends in my personal life before I go.

In the beginning I said this wasn't an autobiography, but you probably knew that wasn't going to be completely true. Obviously, there has been a whole lot of my own story told throughout the entirety of the book, but it was the only way I could make the points I wanted to make.

Our lives are our schools and I've learned what I know primarily through my own experiences.

My purpose in writing what I'm about to write is to hopefully bring a little closure in some areas concerning my coming out and how it has (or may have) affected the people in my life.

But for the most part it's an economical way to answer a lot of the questions I've been asked over the last many months.

Some of these things I've already said to these people in person, and still some may never read these words, but this is something I need to do for a number of reasons...

Here goes...

To My Parents

I want you both to know that I love you very much and am so glad that you're both still here with me, especially after all we've been through together. I'm particularly pleased that you have each other at this time in your lives, because if ever two people were and are in love, the two of you certainly have a very powerful romantic connection that no one can deny.

And I'm happy that we're all good with each other at this point on the journey. I wasted a lot of years being really, really angry with both of you because, for most of my life, I bought into what psychiatrists used to believe was the "cause" of same-sex attraction in people...in a word, I pretty much accepted the assumption that you both had made me gay.

The dysfunction in my relationship with each of you for different reasons—Mom's over-involvement in my life coupled with Dad's extreme distance (or at least, my perception of those things)—was sort of "text book" for that particular psychological model (which the mental health community has now abandoned)... and knowing how you both felt about homosexuality, especially in men and especially back in the day, I felt an overwhelming and hopeless frustration that caused years of anxiety and depression in me.

My line of thinking used to be that the negative judgment and rejection of gay people from their parents is the height of injustice, since it was the parents who made them gay in the first place.

Trying not to be gay for both of you...or rather, trying not to be *myself* for both of you...was really the major motivating force for most of my life.

But the GOOD NEWS is that not only has the mental health community completely abandoned the notion that parents make kids gay, I've abandoned it, too.

I don't think that at all now.

Of course 'nurture' does a lot to shape us, but 'nature' is what determines who we are more than anything else, in my opinion.

I absolutely believe now that I was born gay.

I know that I was aware of how I was wired as early as when Dad pastored in Soddy Daisy, which means I had to be around 4 years old, so my orientation couldn't have come from years and years of conditioning from the two of you.

It's just who I am.

It wasn't your 'fault' (even though I hesitate to use that word because I don't think there's anything wrong with me)...

And after all these years, I'm so relieved to know that you know all about me and still love me...and aren't ashamed of me... especially you, Dad.

I didn't choose it.

You didn't make it happen.

It just is what it is.

I look forward to having some years of authentic peace with you both (now that I've come out and the dust from that has settled a bit), and I hope that our example of unconditional love can inspire some sanity among parents of gay kids who are having difficulty accepting those kids.

Most of all, I want us to be friends and just enjoy the time we have left.

Life's too short to waste it in trying to change the inevitable.

Again, you're both awesome parents and I love you...I know my coming out has cost you most of your friends and connections... I can't do anything to change that and I'm dealing with my own enormous loss in that area...but if I've handled anything inappropriately in coming out...if it has embarrassed you in any way...please forgive me and just love me for who I am...for who I really am and have always been.

In the end, love wins and, again, I love you both.

Our latter will be greater than our former!

That's the GOOD NEWS for us!

To Any Of The Girls Or Young Women That I Either Dated Or Was Engaged To Before I Got Married The First Time

Some of you I've heard from since coming out and you have been so gracious and understanding about the whole thing. Thanks so much, ladies...you have a lot of class.

And to all of you, including those of you I haven't heard from (and probably won't), please forgive me if I hurt you in any way...I certainly have no regrets about my life and I hope you don't either.

Please know that when I dated you or asked you to marry me, I was not trying to deceive you in any way into marrying a gay man. I was doing everything in my power to be the (straight) man that everyone expected me to be (and who I thought God demanded that I be)...and I sincerely believed that I was doing the right thing at the time.

I hope at this point that you realize that not marrying me was obviously the right thing for you (if you even regret it at all... I don't know how to say that without sounding presumptuous) and that you found the right man for your life and that you've been happy.

All's well that ends well and, even if we had a painful break-up, it was for the best.

I'm willing to assume the responsibility for all of it.

Thanks for some great memories and I hope you enjoyed all the dates and the fun we had together and all the nice places I took you and the jewelry you kept after we broke up...no hard feelings at all...

You're all beautiful and sweet and you each added something good to my life...and I hope I added something good to yours...

In fact...ALL things work together for our good!

That's the GOOD NEWS for us!

To My First Wife, Terri

I come in peace.

I hope you're doing well, and I also hope that if and when you read this, you'll understand why I'm addressing you here in this way, and be OK with it. At this point in our lives we really shouldn't have anything to hide or regret, and so I'm believing you'll receive my words in the spirit in which they are intended.

Maybe this will help you get some closure on our relationship, as well.

During my little media blitz when I first came out, some interviewers would ask me about you and about what you thought about my publicly telling the truth about myself, and I never gave them an answer because we've never discussed it.

I've wanted to talk to you about it for a very long time, but I not only know how you feel about gay people, I also know you think that it's a choice—one that you can't comprehend—and when someone thinks that, there's very little that I can say to them concerning the reality of what it means to be gay that would make any real sense to them.

In one phone message that you left me early on after my public coming out, you insisted that someone had just convinced me that I was gay for their own agenda and purposes, and I can only hope that you don't really believe that.

Why would a man like me say it if it weren't true?

I would have absolutely nothing to gain by it.

No one outed me.

It wasn't a response to a scandal.

And no one has or could have that kind of power over me to "convince" me to tell the world that I'm a homosexual if I really weren't!

Initially, I thought you would be relieved to hear that I had come out, because it would mean that you did the right thing in divorcing me all those years ago, even though you didn't do it because of my orientation...I thought it would help you finally make peace with that. Or maybe you have already made peace with it...I don't know. But I think we've both had to deal with a lot of regret for different reasons.

I suppose if you hadn't divorced me, I probably would have eventually filed for divorce, myself, because we caused each other a lot of pain back then.

I guess it really doesn't matter now.

We were very young then, and that was a long time ago.

The GOOD NEWS is that we are in the now, and reconciliation is possible because anything is possible, regardless of how things appear. I'm open to finally having some kind of authentic relationship with you in which we can tell each other the truth without fear of repercussion.

As I said, we've never discussed the truth of my orientation, and every time I've started to approach you about it in the last couple of years, you've either left me a message or sent one through the kids that let me know it probably was premature to try to do so.

To everything there is a season.

Mom had some old, family movie videos put on DVD recently and gave them to me, and I watched them all the other night... they were of you and me when we first got married, some of when Jared was first born, and a little of when Christina was a baby. I hadn't seen them in many, many years and I was taken with how beautiful you were then and how happy we appeared to be when he was first born.

I don't want to believe that none of that was real.

I also want you to know that it was never my intention to defraud you in any way when we got married. I think we both felt a lot of pressure to get together from the people close to us in the church and from our families but, as for me, it was a decision that I made, and so I own it.

I honestly thought as a young man that if I could just fall in love with a woman and get married and have a sex-life with her (I had never really had anything that I would actually call sex with anyone when we got married, male or female), that the same-sex attraction that I had been aware of for my entire life would eventually dissipate.

But even though I could wrap my head around heterosexual intimacy enough to pull it off when I was very young and virile (and when I wanted children), when I finally had it, it only made it clearer than ever that I was absolutely gay.

That kind of connection with a woman never really felt physically natural or emotionally fulfilling to me, and that's not in any way your fault. The fact that being married to you confirmed to me that I was, indeed, gay was more about me than it was about you. You've had a lot of men in your life since our marriage, so obviously you're desirable...you don't need my endorsement for that.

But I did love you and I did always want children, and I know you did, too...so I will never regret marrying you.

I do wish we could have at least have been friends during or after our marriage. I guess I always assumed you suspected that I was really gay on some level, which I thought accounted somewhat for our constant fighting.

But even though we had a rough few years together, because we had Jared and Christina from that union, I don't feel that the time with you was at all wasted.

I hope you feel the same.

Both of them are awesome and I love them so much, as I know you do. They make our short, rocky marriage make sense. And now we even have grandkids together, which I see as a happy ending to it all.

Watching those vids the other night gave me a lot to think about, to say the least...but I choose to remember you the way you were in them, in our early days together when there wasn't so much discord between us...the way you looked and acted in those videos...young and beautiful and excited about motherhood...and I'm glad that after some unfortunate relationships in your life, you finally found someone who really seems to be compatible with you. It seems that you have at last found love with him.

I sincerely hope that you are enjoying some well-deserved happiness in your life now.

God restores the years that the canker worm ate away!

That's the GOOD NEWS for us!

To My Children:
Jared, Christina, Judah and Jonah

There aren't adequate words to express how much I love you, how proud I am of each of you, and how much you all make my life make sense. You are the four most wonderful and amazing people in the world, as far as I'm concerned, and I am blessed to be your father.

I pray for you every day, and I thank God for you every day.

I know so many gay men, and have even dated a few, who always wanted children, and still want them—just because you're gay doesn't mean you don't have paternal instincts (maternal for lesbians)—and each one of them has told me how envious he is of what I have with you.

Sometimes I think I should have just come out when I was a young man and lived my truth, but you know I don't do regrets...

If I had come out back in the day, I wouldn't have gotten married and I wouldn't have you.

You make all of it worth it.

Christina, I came out to you first and I will never forget how supportive and understanding you were that night. You'll always be my little girl, but that night you were such a strong and mature woman...a rock for me...I really felt like you became my friend at that moment and you gave me the courage to believe I could tell the boys. You're still a great friend...and a wonderful mother...and an awesome person... and I love you so much...more than you could ever know.

Judah and Jonah, I dreaded telling you guys about myself more than anyone else for some reason...just never wanted to embarrass you or make you think I wasn't great. It's always been so important to me that you have a high opinion of me and I never wanted to do anything that would tarnish that image. But after your mom filed for divorce, I knew I had to tell you the real reason for the break-up. You guys deserved the truth and I appreciate that she left it to me to tell you.

In many ways, I think our divorce was harder on you than my coming out was.

But that night you guys were both so compassionate and understanding. I'll never forget it. I think if one or both of you had freaked out on me that night, I probably wouldn't have made it. I was already in a dark place, and that would have been the end for me.

Not trying to sound dramatic...it's just the truth.

And if you had asked me not to come out publicly, I honestly don't know if I ever would have.

But your support and humor and faithfulness and maturity and friendship have just blown me away.

Don't know what I'd do without you guys.

And Jared, you were out of the country, as usual, so I came out to you over the phone when you were at the Paris airport... never did see how much that phone bill was...I just remember it was the most powerful and intense conversation I've ever had with you in my or your life. Your words of love and support that night are burned into my brain.

And a few weeks later, the letter you wrote me encouraging me to come out publicly was really the thing that gave me the strength to finally do it.

I've read it a thousand times and refer to it often.

And then, a few days after that, when Jared got back to the states, the five of us went out to dinner (it was Father's Day) and then went to Piedmont Park and sat at one of the picnic tables and talked about it all. I had come out to each of you separately, but wanted to talk about it with all of you together without interruption.

It was one of the most beautiful nights of my life and I never felt closer to any of you than I did sitting in that park for those hours. Your words saved my life and I can hardly believe how blessed I am to have you.

I like to think that you're all as proud of me as I am of you...at least that's what I hope.

There aren't enough words to appropriately apologize to each of you for the fact that you all now have had to endure the divorce of your parents...I do have intense sorrow for that and wish there was a way I could spare you from the pain of it...but it is what it is...

If I thought about it too much, it would overwhelm me...

But I want you all to know that you have and will always have my unconditional love and support for anything you ever do, and I have the utmost confidence that you all will do well.

I love you with my life.

Great shall be the peace and undisturbed composure of my children!

That's the GOOD NEWS for us!

To Debye

I know that a lot of people don't understand the nature of our unusual relationship...sometimes I don't fully understand it myself, either...but I know that love is complicated, and that I love you and always will.

I'm especially grateful that we both have people in our lives now who love us enough to make room for our very rare, synergistic connection...that they understand that love and accept it for what it is. I won't mention either of them by name to respect their privacy, and because I don't know what the future holds for any of us, but it seems at this juncture that we have both been blessed with relationships with two good, decent and mature men who apparently are supernaturally equipped to deal with our "thing" and with being a part of our "modern family." You've been with yours considerably longer than I've been with mine, but so far, so good.

God is good!

It's *all* good!

I've said all of this to you already, but I still don't doubt that God brought us together and I have no regrets about our time together or our marriage.

After my first divorce, I never thought that I would attempt marriage again. I just planned to be married to God and try to be a good father. At the time, I had my hands full with a young, growing church and having Jared and Christina three days a week, so I just intended on pouring my energy into dealing with all of that, especially because the kids were so little at the time...Christina was just a baby.

But when I met you, something real happened between us that is still difficult to explain to people. I'm not bisexual–I don't even really believe in bisexuality, personally–but something definitely happened with us that was a genuine love between a man and a woman, strange as that seems to say. That's why, when I saw that it was getting serious between us, I went ahead and told you that, even though I didn't act on it, I knew I was gay.

I didn't want to complicate anyone else's life and assumed that you would react to my disclosure by choosing to just be my very good friend.

But you told me that you were in love with me, and I felt like I was in love with you, so we got married.

I think on some level we believed, at least subconsciously, that we could change me.

Of course, we both know now that we were attempting the impossible.

But even though our relationship became platonic after Jonah was born, it continued to grow and deepen over the years, which is why I know we never felt like it was a sham marriage. It might not have been conventional in the sense of how marriages are supposed to go, but it was real for us...it wasn't an "arrangement."

I think that I can safely speak for both of us in what I'm about to say, since we've discussed these things so many times, but several factors have contributed to making our 22-year marriage so strong and our current relationship so unbreakable.

First, we've always liked each other. We might not have enjoyed intimacy as other married couples do, but I'm sure no one has had a better time together than we have.

You instantly became a wonderful mom to my very young kids as soon as we got married, and then we had two of our own... and we have always enjoyed our kids.

We built a mega-ministry together that made a real difference in peoples' lives and throughout the world...and still does.

We enjoyed so many of the same things.

We bought and sold houses and decorated and re-decorated them...and made a little money off of them.

We traveled around the world.

We enjoyed some of the finer things of life as the ministry grew and we became prosperous.

We laughed a lot.

We had a lot of fun.

And then there were outside, antagonistic forces that forged a strong bond between us as well—the denomination that I was a part of when I met you ex-communicating me for being "doubly married"...years and years of intense drama with my ex-wife and her husbands...the religious community who never understood what we were about, even before I came out—all of these things together sort of created a 'you and me against the world' mindset that I think we still have...

But, even though we rarely discussed it, the elephant in the room was always there.

We both knew I was a gay man and that, apparently, I would always be, whether or not I was ever actually in a relationship with a man or not. I thought that you would have left me years before you did—especially because we were really more like roommates than a married couple in a lot of ways—but when you didn't, I eventually just assumed that we would go the distance together because I never planned on coming out.

But one night. after a season of some unexpected turbulence between us, you confronted me with my own life's message: REAL PEOPLE, EXPERIENCING THE REAL GOD IN THE REAL WORLD...in that conversation you said, "You tell everyone else to be real and that God loves them just as they are, but you don't even give yourself the same grace."

Those words changed everything.

When you finally told me that you were divorcing me after 20 plus years, I asked you not to do it, even though I knew you weren't doing it to hurt me. You said that I should come out. I insisted that I never would...that we would lose everything we had worked for if I did...that you were underestimating the power of homophobia.

You insisted that I was underestimating the people in my life.

As it turns out, we were both right, and we were both wrong.

Homophobia is a big deal, as we soon discovered, and we did, in fact, lose a lot because of it.

A whole lot.

But the people in our lives—those in whom we had invested so much time and energy, along with my parents and your parents and, of course, the kids—really did rise to the occasion and grow with us, and so we still have a life and a ministry and relationships that have been tried in the fire and have come forth as pure gold.

Apparently, I had underestimated the sophistication and enlightenment of some of the people in my/our life.

So, thank you for having the courage to divorce me.

I don't know that I would have ever come out if you hadn't...at least not as long as my parents were alive.

But you did the right thing.

And I know you love me, and I know you know that I love you.

And you've never looked more beautiful than you do now...I'm glad you have the love of a straight man...you deserve it...you seem very happy.

I've written a lot of great things about you in previous books, and none of the things I said in those pages was a lie.

You really are an amazing woman.

I've meant every good word I've ever said about you.

Thanks for believing in me and for submitting to that word we received many years ago that we would do something that has never been done before.

He does exceeding, abundantly above all we can ask or think!

That's the GOOD NEWS for us!

To All The People Who Instantly Exited My Life When I Came Out And Completely Cut Me Off

I could say a lot about friendship...about loyalty...about having been a good pastor and bishop to you...about being a good friend to you...about deserving better from you...about covering you and keeping things in confidence for you over the years...

I could say "you're welcome" for multiplied thousands upon tens of thousands of dollars I invested in your ministries over the many years...for supporting you...for sitting with you in hospital rooms and bailing you out of jails and going with you to pick out burial plots for your loved ones...for visiting your sick family members...for hardly ever being out of the pulpit for decades and for picking up the phone when you called for prayer at three in the morning...or paying your light bills and your mortgage payments...

I could say "you're welcome" for honoraria I paid you to speak at my church...love offerings that were twice my salary (even though you pretend now that you never knew me)...

I could say, "Seriously? After 25, 30 years, not even a phone call or letter? Not even a good-bye?"

I could say, "How's that tongue thing working out for you?" to those of you who said, "May my tongue cleave to the roof of my mouth if I ever say anything negative about you" while we took communion together...

I could use words like fear, homophobia, over-reaction, immaturity, intolerance...

...hypocrisy, legalism, religious spirit, for those of you who one moment called me the most anointed man you ever met... your spiritual father...a man of revelation...and in the next minute called me a reprobate...

I could think about how you jumped ship and simply say, "Wow..."

But what would be the point?

I forgive you and release you...

All things are naked and open unto the eyes of Him with whom we have to do...

That's the GOOD NEWS for me!

To My God

Lord, you know all and see all...

You are God, and beside you there is no other...

You know my downsitting and my uprising...there is not a word in my tongue that you don't know, altogether...

I've loved you my whole life and tried to serve you as best I knew how.

Only you know the prayers I prayed and the tears I cried my whole life concerning the truth of my life.

Only you know how I have made peace now with who I am...with who You made me to be...

If I've said anything in this book that is wrong, please forgive me and let the words fall to the ground.

If you are the God that the legalists and fundamentalists say you are, then there is no hope me...or for any of us for that matter...

If I'm wrong about the Gospel...if it's not the GOOD NEWS that I believe it really is...then forgive me for that, too, and let anything I've said about it that is wrong also fall to the ground.

But if you really are as good as I believe you are...if you really are love, as the Scriptures say you are, then please bless this book and all who read it...

If the GOOD NEWS is real, as I believe it is, then let everything that can be shaken be shaken, and let that GOOD NEWS be published and proclaimed all over the earth!

I pray for mercy on us all...

I pray for favor on this book and that it will help someone...

Let Your Kingdom come, let Your will be done on earth as it is in heaven...

Our God is an awesome God, and that's

GOOD NEWS!

Peace to you all!

GLOSSARY OF TERMS

BAPTISM IN/OF THE HOLY SPIRIT: A spiritual experience originating from Trinitarian Pentecostal or Charismatic theology, based on the events of the second chapter of the Book of Acts. It is referred to as 'a second work of grace' by these groups, subsequent to the New Birth, as they define it. The approach of the Charismatics to this experience was and is somewhat different from that of the classical Pentecostals, but the result is the same...an enduement of spiritual power (Acts 1:8) with the 'official, physical evidence' being the gift of "speaking with other tongues" (Acts 2:4).

FUNDAMENTALISM, FUNDAMENTALIST: A movement in American Protestantism that arose in the early part of the twentieth century in reaction to modernism that stresses the infallibility of the Bible, not only in matters of faith and morals, but also as a literal, historical record, holding as essential to Christian faith a belief in such doctrines as the creation of the world in six literal earth-days.

HOMOPHOBIA: (from Wikipedia) A range of negative attitudes and feelings toward homosexuality or people who are identified or perceived as being lesbian, gay, bisexual or transgender (LGBT). Definitions refer variably to antipathy, contempt, prejudice, aversion, irrational fear, and hatred. In a 1998 address, author, activist and civil rights leader Coretta Scott King stated that "Homophobia is like racism and anti-Semitism and other forms of bigotry in that it seeks to dehumanize a large group of people, to deny their humanity, their dignity and personhood."

Homophobia is observable in critical and hostile behavior such as discrimination and violence on the basis of sexual orientations that are non-heterosexual. According to the 2010 Hate Crimes Statistics released by the FBI National Press Office, 19.3 percent of hate crimes across the United States "were motivated by a sexual orientation bias." Moreover, a Southern Poverty Law Center 2010 *Intelligence Report* extrapolating data from 14 years (1995–2008) (which had complete data available at the time) of the FBI's national hate crime statistics, found that LGBT people were "far more likely than any other minority group in the United States to be victimized by violent hate crime."

Recognized types of homophobia include *institutionalized* homophobia (e.g., religious homophobia and state-sponsored homophobia) and *internalized* homophobia, experienced by people who have same-sex attractions, regardless of how they identify. Forms of homophobia toward identifiable LGBT social groups have similar yet specific names.

LEGALISM, LEGALISTIC: Legalism is a strict, literal adherence to the law or to a particular code, as of religion or morality. In the Biblical interpretation sense, legalism particularly exalts the letter of a passage above the spirit of it, often completely ignoring context, poetic language, allegory or any sense of the abstract.

"THE RAPTURE": A term not found in the Bible, was coined by John Nelson Darby (1800–1882), the man who originated the doctrine of a two-part, literal return of Jesus Christ to the earth in bodily form. **"The Rapture"** (from the same Latin root as **rape**: *to seize someone and take them away),* according to Darby and the way he interpreted certain Scriptures and connected them together, happens seven years prior to the Second Coming of Christ and is a literal event when the Christians of the earth will be teleported to another celestial location for a number of years before returning to the earth with Jesus Christ. **"The Great Tribulation,"** according to this interpretation, is the time between these two events when the world will experience horrible and extreme manifestations of the wrath of God.

WITNESSING: Personal evangelism, done on a one-on-one basis.

REFERENCES

"One Thing I Can Tell You Is, You Got To Be Free" – lyrics from The Beatles' song entitled, *Come Together*

"This is My Story, This is My Song" – song written by Fanny Crosby

"And Now For The Rest Of The Story" – Paul Harvey (taken from his radio program entitled, *The Rest of the Story*)

"I Want To Thank You For Lettin' Me Be Myself Again" – song recorded by Sly and the Family Stone

"Jesus is Just Alright with Me" –gospel song lyrics written by Arthur Reid Reynolds, secularly recorded by The Doobie Brothers, as well as other artists

"Oh, How I Love Jesus" – song written by Frederick Whitfield, 1829–1904

"Don't Worry, Be Happy" – song written by Robert "Bobby" McFerrin, Jr.

"Come Fly With Me" – song written for Frank Sinatra by Jimmy Van Heusen, with lyrics by Sammy Cahn

"No Hell Below Us, Above Us Only Sky" – lyrics from the song entitled, *Imagine;* written and performed by John Lennon

"Bad Boys, Bad Boys, Whatcha Gonna Do?" – song written by Inner Circle

"It's a Puzzlement" – quote from Yul Brenner, from the movie, *The King and I*

"You Can't Handle the Truth!" – from the movie, *A Few Good Men*

"Who Wrote the Book of Love?" – song recorded by The Monotones in 1957, which was written by three members of the group: Warren Davis, George Malone and Charles Patrick. It became the theme song of *The Newlywed Game*.

"Lift Every Voice and Sing" – song written by James Johnson, 1899; aka *"The Negro National Hymn."*

"We Gotta Get Out Of This Place" – song written by Barry Mann and Cynthia Weil; recorded in 1965 by The Animals

"Why Don't We All Just Get Stoned?" – song written and performed by Jimmy Buffett

"The Sound Of Silence" – song written by Paul Simon, performed by Simon and Garfunkel

"Listen To What The Man Said" – 1975 hit single recorded by Paul McCartney and Wings

"You're A Mean One, Mr. Grinch" – lyrics from the movie based on the Dr. Seuss book entitled, *How the Grinch Stole Christmas*

"You Better Think" – lyrics from Aretha Franklin's song, *Think*

"In the Beginning" – Genesis 1:1, The Holy Bible

"Momma Always Said, 'Stupid Is As Stupid Does.'" – quote from the movie, *Forrest Gump*.

"I Always Feel Like Somebody's Watching Me" – lyrics from the 1984 song entitled, *Somebody's Watching Me,* by Rockwell.

"What's Love Got To Do With It?" – Tina Turner song title released June 4, 1984.

"Your Own Personal Jesus" – lyrics from the U.K.'s Depeche Mode's single entitled, *Personal Jesus,* released in 1989

"We Shall Overcome" – from the song entitled, *"I'll Overcome Someday,"* written by Rev. Charles Albert Tindley and published in 1901. The song later became the protest anthem of the African-American civil rights movement from 1955-1968.

"What's Goin' On?" – Marvin Gaye song, released in 1971

"There's A New World Coming" – lyrics from the song, *New World Coming,* performed by Mama Cass Elliot

"What The World Needs Now Is Love" – 1965 song with lyrics by Hal Davis and music composed by Burt Bacharach, was first recorded by Jackie DeShannon

"Ain't That GOOD NEWS? – song written and released in 1964, performed by soul singer, Sam Cooke

"I Will Always Love You" – song written by country music artist Dolly Parton and recorded first in 1973. Whitney Houston recorded a version of the song for the 1992 film, *The Bodyguard.*

Other books by Bishop Swilley . . .

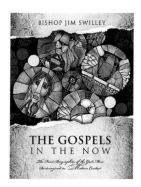

The Gospels In The Now

The Four Biographies of the God-Man Re-Imagined in Modern Context

Why read a new paraphrase of the Gospels? If you've been previously intimidated or confused or bored by the Bible, regardless of its available translations and paraphrases, then this book will make you more comfortable with it and with your own interpretations and opinions about it. The Bible is hearty and robust, not delicate or fragile; it can withstand a lot of handling by human beings because it was meant to be people-friendly. This paraphrase celebrates the conflicting viewpoints of the writers with their different paradigms of God and will help you rediscover and rethink the Gospels. And, it will help you know and love Jesus—the God-man Who cannot be bound or limited in any way by religion or philosophy or doctrines or dogma...the firstborn among many siblings in the family of God who live in the twenty-first century—the Christ, better. It will open a door to the house of understanding and let you in!

Excerpts from *The Gospels In The Now*

But seek out and search for a revelation of the Kingdom of God in and through every circumstance, and in every situation. And seek it first (or first thing)...before you strive with the circumstance...before you start to worry about the situation...before you fret over it...before you allow yourself to become overwhelmed by it or let it become exaggerated in your mind.

(Matthew 6:33 – Matthew In The Now)

This is why I am telling you, whatever you ask for in prayer...whatever you decree...BELIEVE...accept the reality that it exists in another, unseen dimension, simply because you say it. Don't suspend or delay belief until you see it manifested in the physical realm, because what is unseen is more real than what is seen. Be confident that your request is granted to you, and you will get it...your own irresistible faith will attract it to you.

(Mark 11:24 – Mark In The Now)

And give...give generously and freely...because if you do, gifts will be lavished upon you...and these gifts will be abundant (to demonstrate the infinite possibilities of the Kingdom), packed down (to make room for more), shaken together (to make sure that you never receive filler), and running all over the place (so that you never have a sense of lack)! People will come into your life just to give to you, and this is the way that they will pour into the pouch formed by the bosom of your robe and used as a bag. You define your own terms in this, for with the same measure you deal out—with the measure you use when you confer benefits on others—it will be measured back to you!

(Luke 6:38 – Luke In The Now)

You see, God's love for the whole world—His paternal affection for the entire cosmos—was so all-encompassing and complete that He freely gave His unique Son to it, so that anyone from that world who believes in Him would not perish but would awaken to the fact that eternal life is theirs. It certainly was never God's intention to send His Son into the world to pronounce a sentence of condemnation upon it. Rather, He was perfectly focused on saving it...on redeeming the whole of humanity...everyone and everything on the planet...through the gift of that unique, manifested Son.

(John 3:16, 17 – John In The Now)

God is always now, and my prayer is that as you read The Gospels In The Now you will walk in a fuller revelation of that. **Now** is all that matters!

– Bishop Jim Swilley

A Year In The Now

a dynamic devotional dedicated to the daily discovery of destiny

Would you like to . . .

> . . . discover your destiny?
> . . . perceive your purpose?
> . . . validate your vision?
> . . . reinforce your relationships?
> . . . strengthen your self-esteem?
> . . . overcome your obstacles?
> . . . feed your faith?

> You can . . . this year!
> You can . . . by living in the now!
> You can . . . one day at a time!

God is on your side! He is available to assist you in the pursuit of your potential as you develop the diligence to seriously search out your personal path for growth into greatness! Through seeking first His Kingdom and righteousness, you can become the person that He created you to be!

You can ONLY find God's Kingdom in the eternal NOW as you endeavor to experience Him in your everyday existence. Kingdom-seeking consists of a constant effort to embrace the "now" and a commitment to the continual conforming of your consciousness to it. This empowers and enables you to escape the mental distractions produced by living in the past or in the future, so that you can comprehend a real Christ for your current real circumstances!

A YEAR IN THE NOW! is a devotional designed to deliver a doable format for the daily development of your eternal life—to help you think creatively, beyond your familiar, time-bound comfort zones. These positive and powerful affirmations will provide the help you need to progressively put your life on the right track in realistic increments. You don't have to become overwhelmed by the tremendous task of trying to lead a *now life* in a *yesterday/tomorrow world*. You can do it day by day!

This is your year to change your world! You can change your world by changing your mind! You can change your mind one day at a time! It's time for a fresh start, and you can start right NOW!

What others have to say about *A Year In The Now*...

When my dear friend, Bishop Jim Swilley sent me a copy... I stopped everything I was doing and couldn't put it down...Jim is one of the most effective, prolific, and unique communicators I have ever met. He breaks down deep and profound truth and makes it palatable for all of us in such a practical way that just reading the principles and reciting the affirmations increases our life skills. The days are broken down into seven key principles a day, seven being the number of alignment between heaven and earth (four being the number of earth, and three of heaven), whereby applying the seven daily truths your heart and mind are aligned with heaven's best and you are automatically brought into the kind of agreement that gets results in your life. If you want to get the "more" out of your daily life that has been promised to you in Christ I want to encourage you to get your hands on *A Year In The Now!* and make it a part of your daily spiritual discipline and focus.

Dr. Mark J. Chironna
The Master's Touch International Church

A Year in the Now! reads as a personal message to me. Each day I am encouraged—God is doing a new thing in the NOW...This devotional reinforces that God is working His plan in all things....

Germaine Copeland
Author of Prayers That Avail Much Family Books

Deeply profound, yet 'DO-ably' practical...Bishop Jim's 'easy to read' style of communication, combined with his witty grouping together of words that start with the same letter, define this devotional as a delightful way to delve deeper into your divine destiny as a daily discipline. Profound and practical, it's the perfect proponent to promote your personal progress.

Doug Fortune
Trumpet Call Ministry

*A Year In The Now!.*is extraordinary and powerful, giving day by day guidance on how to be strong in the Lord through seven pearls of wisdom each day. Seven! This is God's number for completeness and fulfillment. Through *A Year In The Now!*, God is truly using Bishop Swilley in a mighty way to unlock the wonderful mystery of the gospel so that each of us can live abundantly and serve God abundantly, in the now!

David Scott
United States Congressman, Georgia

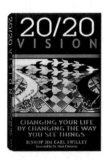

20/20 VISION

Changing Your Life
By Changing The Way You See Things

You really can live a larger life, starting now, by increasing your vision and improving your personal perception and your perception of the world around you. *20/20 VISION* is based on 20 daily affirmations that you can make concerning how you see yourself, and another 20 daily affirmations that you can make concerning how you see everything else. Each affirmation has commentary that expounds on its meaning for your life, with a plan to help you observe things in a better light and encourage you to say something good about what you see every day.

You can, in fact, change your life by changing the way that you see things. It has been theorized that there is no such thing as *reality,* there is only *perception*—a premise that can be argued, ad infinitum, by philosophers and physicists, alike. Whether or not it is actually and completely true, the fact remains that your perception of things really does determine how you think, feel and function every single day of your life. It is a fact that God *is,* but it is also a fact that God is to you how you *see* that He is.

You can determine your own happiness by learning how to properly view and discern the circumstances of your past and present. By learning how to see yourself correctly, you can become the person you've always really wanted to be or, better yet, you can reveal the best "you" that you already are. You have the ability to choose an attitude and vision for each day with the same confidence and ease that you have when choosing what to have for breakfast in the morning or what clothes to wear for the day. The more you are able to see how inner sight creates daily realities, the better skilled you will become in using it to your advantage.

Free your mind, open the eyes of your heart and prepare to change your life for the better. You **can** be happy. You **can** succeed. You **can** stop second-guessing your life choices, living in regret or blaming others. You **can** break all the limitations of your own mind and tap into an inner power that will enable you to do things that you never thought you could do before. And you can do it all by simply choosing to change your viewpoint and perception of the things pertaining to your life. As you begin to realize personal transformation, let these words take on new meaning for you: *I once was lost, but now am found; was blind, but now I see!*

[A separate 20/20 VISION Workbook is also available.]

What others have to say about *20/20 VISION...*

My friend, Bishop Jim Swilley, has written this masterpiece...and it is a sure invitation to a larger life by making that fundamental shift in your perception of reality. If you ever doubted whether God had more in store for you, this book will change your paradigm forever. Let the words of this book give you the permission you need to open the windows of your perception, change the way you view yourself and the world you live and, and watch both you and that world undergo incredible and remarkable transformation!

---Dr. Mark J. Chironna
Mark Chironna Ministries
www.markchironna.com

My friend, Jim Swilley, has successfully entered the marketplace of visualization and given correct spiritual understanding of a principle that literally creates success or failure, life or death, poverty or prosperity...Jim's book will change the lives of millions of people because he is adding vision to their sight.

---Prophet Kim Clement
Prophetic Image Expressions

In a way that only he can, Bishop Jim Swilley has taken the principles of Scripture and made them practical and doable. *20/20 VISION* challenges its readers to elevate their perception from being down-trodden, victimized and hopeless, to being empowered, capable and victorious....

---Bishop Eddie L. Long
Senior Pastor, New Birth Missionary Baptist Church

Bishop Swilley has done it again! His ability to provide daily insights for life is simply amazing...*20/20* is a must read for every believer!

---Pastor Dony McGuire
The River at Music City

Bishop Swilley shows us how we often view ourselves through lenses clouded by hurt, unforgiveness, bitterness and self-doubt. He reveals how we see ourselves through the lenses of others and believe that mirage, instead of the divine reality and purpose God has ordained for us.

---Minister Steen "Newslady" Miles
Senator, State of Georgia

Twenty-Three

New Reflections on the 23rd Psalm and You

The beautifully simple lyrics to David's timeless masterpiece remain as life-affirming and culturally relevant today as they were thousands of years ago when he originally wrote them.

In this accessible, topical devotional based on his song that we know as the 23rd Psalm, you will find a positive "now" word for your every situation. You will want to keep a copy handy at all times to remind you that you can live fearlessly, even when walking through your own valley of the shadow of death. And when you are stressed out or feeling intimidated by those who try to oppose you, you will find in these pages the grace to help you lie down in green pastures and the encouragement to eat at the very table that the Shepherd has prepared for you in the presence of your enemies. His rod and His staff will comfort you at all times, and *Twenty-Three* will help you to use that rod and staff more effectively and to enjoy a more fulfilling life as you learn to dwell in the house of the Lord forever.

From the Foreword: *"I wholeheartedly endorse both this book and the author. You will be encouraged, edified and uplifted with nothing but the good news. Bishop Swilley is a breath of fresh air in the religious climate of pretentiousness and egotism."*
— Bishop David Huskins

JOHN IN THE NOW

THE GOSPEL OF ST. JOHN
RE-IMAGINED IN MODERN CONTEXT

John's account of the greatest story ever told is in a class all by itself. It is the gospel written for nonconformists and individualists—for those who can comprehend Jesus outside the box

JITN will help you open your mind to a side of the real Jesus that you may not have noticed was there before. *An audio version of John In The Now (read by Bishop Swilley) is also available.*

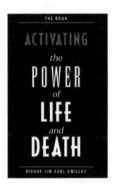

Activating the Power of Life and Death

It's your life . . .
It's your choice . . .
YOU CHOOSE!

God has given you the power to choose life or death, blessing or cursing. By the words of your mouth, you determine the quality of your life. This powerful book will help put you in charge of your life and your future.

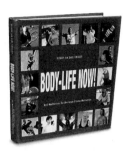

Body-Life Now!

Mini-Meditations for Maximum Fitness Motivation

Whether you're a serious body builder, competitive athlete, or just somebody who wants to drop a few pounds and be a little healthier than you are now, this power-devotional is for you! Inside you'll find 75 crisp little meditations on fitness, nutrition, attitude and lifestyle that will supercharge your workout and improve your outlook on your day.

You'll be doing yourself a big favor by incorporating these inspiring pages into your regular routine, *however* you choose to do so. Your spirit will be refreshed, your mind will be sharpened, and your body will thank you for the extra empowerment.

And if you're just getting *started* on the road to physical fitness, you'll find this book to be *especially* beneficial. It will serve as an easy-to-read road map for the journey designed to help you discover the new, improved *you*.

That journey can start right *here*...and it can start right *NOW!*

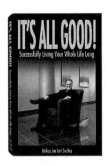

It's All Good!

Successfully Living Your *Whole* Life Long

Pursuing peace with your **past** . . .
Perceiving purpose in your **present** . . .
Fearlessly facing your **future** . . .

All these themes *and more* are explored in this provocative study of the powerful implications of Romans 8:28:

> *And we know that all things work together for good to those who love God, to those who are the called according to His purpose.*

Balancing the *secular* with the *sacred*, this candidly autobiographical and brutally honest book will make you *laugh* and make you *think*.

More importantly, it will help you begin to see how the plan for your life is unfolding every day and how God's "big picture" is revealing your destiny.

Every page contains good news and vital information about how to successfully live your **whole life long**. It's all here, and *it's all good!*

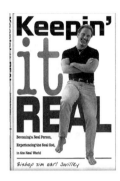

Keepin' It Real

Becoming a Real Person, Experiencing the Real God, in the Real World

You've never read a book quite like *Keepin' It Real!* In its pages, Bishop Swilley candidly examines an unusually wide array of subjects...the reality TV phenomenon... pop culture... history...politics...self-esteem...prosperity... success... parenting...multiculturalism...New Age philosophy... world religions...political correctness...racism...sexism... tolerance... activism...technology...addiction...eschatology... dispensationalism...the antichrist...orthodoxy...prayer...the Holy Spirit... destiny...purpose...vision...and much more...and addresses how they all relate to the Kingdom of God in the now!

But *Keepin' it Real* is also about *you* and how you can develop the courage and confidence to be yourself at all times and to live your *real* life without compromise. Socially relevant, thought-provoking, and theologically edgy, *Keepin' it Real* is a modern manifesto for REAL PEOPLE EXPERIENCING THE REAL GOD IN THE REAL WORLD.®

If you're ready to get *real*, get this book!

School of the Bible Seminar Materials:

The School of the Bible seminars were one day meetings consisting of four to five sessions. In these sessions, Bishop Jim presents ideas about ancient truths for your consideration and answers some questions that have been asked of him. Above all, everything discussed in this material must be potentially summed up in these three words: **God Is Love!** This and all Gospel preaching/teaching must meet that criterion. If it doesn't demonstrate and exalt the love of God, it's not the Gospel. (All sessions available on DVD, CD and MP3; a corresponding Workbook is also available.)

School of the Bible I Topics

- How We Got Our Bible
- What is Hell and Who is the Devil?
- Are We Living in the End-Times?
- God's Mercy to All

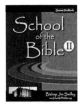

School of the Bible II Topics

- How to Study the Bible
- Overview of the Book of Revelation
- The Lake of Fire and the Second Death
- Christ Is All and Is In All: The
- Greatness of God

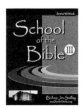

School of the Bible III Topics

- The Gospel of the Kingdom: Developing a Real Theology for Real People Living in the Real World
- A Global Vision: Understanding Christ and World Religions
- The Restoration of All Things: Understanding the Doctrine of Universal Reconciliation
- On Earth as it is in Heaven: The Manifestation of the Unconditional Love of God

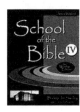

School of the Bible IV Topics

- Behold the Lamb of God Who Takes Away the Sin of the World
- The Mark of the Lamb: Overcoming the Worship of the Beast
- Singing the "Uni-Verse": Global Reconciliation Revealed in the Psalms
- The Songs of Revelation: John's Vision of Universal Worship

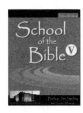

School of the Bible V Topics

- Rightly Dividing the Scriptures
- The Letter Kills: Bible History and the Religious Roots of Racism
- The Letter Kills: Bible History, Sexism, and the Liberation of Women
- The Letter Kills: Tracing the Roots of Homophobia
- But the Spirit Gives Life: A Study in the Work of the Holy Spirit in Reconciliation

Washed by the Word Music Products: (the spoken Word over a background of live, instrumental music)

A distinctive quality of Bishop Swilley is his frequent practice of quoting Scripture and washing his congregation with the mind-renewing, life-changing Word of God. Finally, after many requests, the *Washed by the Word* series was recorded live at Church In The Now. You will be greatly blessed as you hear the anointed Word spoken into your life and will want to play them over and over again.

Washed by the Word track listing:

In His Presence • The Authority of the Word • The Psalms • The Word Concerning Your Righteousness • Your Blessing for Favor • Your Blessing for Prosperity and Success • The Healing Scriptures • Your Blessing for Peace • The Word Concerning Your Children • Your Blessing for Strength • Your Blessing for Joy • The Word Concerning Your Dreams and Visions • Faith Builders • The Word Concerning Your Destiny and Future • O Magnify the Lord With Me

Washed by the Word AM & PM track listing:

AM: *Morning Has Broken • Good Day Sunshine! • Give Us This Day Our Daily Bread • Carpe Diem! • The Mind of Christ • Attitude Adjustment • Great Expectations • The Whole Armor of God • I Can Do All Things Through Christ • Get In The Groove!*

PM: *Evening Praise • Count Your Blessings • Let It Go • Angels Watching Over Me • No Plague Comes Near My Dwelling • Take No Thought for Tomorrow • Cast All Your Care upon Him • Now I Lay Me Down to Sleep • Sweet Dreams • Sleep in Heavenly Peace*

Washed by the Word for Kids track listing:

Opening Prayer • This is the Day the Lord has Made! • You Are Special! • The Word Concerning Success in School • A Blessing for Girls • A Blessing for Boys • The Word Concerning Your Family • The Word Concerning Your Friends • The Blessing of Obedience • Overcoming Bad Memories • The Word Concerning Your Character • The Word Concerning Your Destiny and Future • Don't be Afraid of the Dark • Peaceful Sleep

For more information on these products,
please visit the website at
www.churchinthenow.org
www.jimswilleybooks.com

For large quantity purchases, please email:
info@churchinthenow.org
info@jimswilleybooks.com